DIY FERMENTATION

DO-IT-YOURSELF FERMENTS

Is the art of fermentation new to you? Get started with these simple DIY ferments and unleash the crafty cook in you.

- Sauerkraut (page 34) will be your trusty fermentation primer. Perfect for first-timers, a jar of homemade kraut will make even the simplest dinners sublime.

- Kimchi (page 39) is a great next step for vegetable ferments. Prepare a batch and enjoy its probiotic benefits as an accompaniment to every meal.

- Looking for a simple fruit ferment? Whip up a batch of Blackberry-Sage Jam (page 65) and jar it for a DIY gift that is sure to please.

- Make your own Kombucha (page 156) and ditch the expensive store-bought bottles.

Happy Fermenting!

KATHERINE GREEN

DIY FERMENTATION

OVER 100 STEP-BY-STEP HOME FERMENTATION RECIPES

in collaboration with

ROCKRIDGE PRESS

For general information on our other products and services or to obtain technical support, please contact our Customer Care Department within the United States at (866) 744-2665, or outside the United States at (510) 253-0500.

Rockridge Press publishes its books in a variety of electronic and print formats. Some content that appears in print may not be available in electronic books, and vice versa.

TRADEMARKS: Rockridge Press and the Rockridge Press logo are trademarks or registered trademarks of Callisto Media Inc. and/or its affiliates, in the United States and other countries, and may not be used without written permission. All other trademarks are the property of their respective owners. Rockridge Press is not associated with any product or vendor mentioned in this book.

Interior photo credits: Shutterstock/Jack Jelly, p. 2 (Left); Stocksy/Canan Czemmel, p. 2 (Right); Shutterstock/Jack Jelly, p. 3; Stockfood/Michael Wissing, p. 6; Stockfood/Keller & Keller Photography, p. 9; Stockfood/Anthony Lanneretonne, p. 10; Stockfood/Teubner Foodfoto GmbH, p. 15; Stockfood/Sabine Löscher, p.15; Stockfood/Pastel Chaudron, p. 18; Shannon Oslick, p.25; Stockfood/José Marie Jarry, p. 29; Stocksy/Alita Ong, p. 30; Stockfood/Michael Wissing, p. 62; Stockfood/Sarka Babicka, p. 76; Stockfood/Oliver Brachat, p. 92; Stocksy/Noemi Hauser, p. 108; Stockfood/Eising Studio – Food Photo & Video, p. 126; Stockfood/Greg Rannells Photography, p. 138; Stockfood/Leigh Beisch, p. 152; Stockfood/Ian Garlick, p. 174; Stockfood/Tony Hurley, p. 192

Cover photo credits: Penny de los Santos/Offset (front cover); Richard Jung Photography/Stockfood (back cover)

Illustrations © 2015 by Tom Bingham

ISBN: Print 978-1-62315-528-5 | eBook 978-1-62315-585-8

CONTENTS

INTRODUCTION

Once upon a time, long before refrigeration allowed us the luxury of planning meals and storing food, fermentation was king. Originally used as a way to preserve foods, fermentation has given us some of the food world's most treasured delights. Coffee, chocolate, cheese, beer, wine, and pickles all make use of this ancient process to transform food from its original state into something extraordinary.

Simply defined as a metabolic process that converts sugars into acid, gas, or alcohol, fermentation can take many forms. Although the standard American diet does not include a wide variety of these foods, many cultures around the world serve fermented food with just about every meal. These items—often raw and living foods teeming with beneficial bacteria—can improve health and vitality. Bonus: They taste great, too!

As early as the third century BC, laborers building the Great Wall of China were served fermented vegetables as part of their daily rations. From there, the tradition spread throughout Asia and Europe, with many far-ranging styles and varieties gaining recognition in different regions.

Fermentation was probably originally developed to help stretch the harvest and provide nourishment when fall changed to winter, but the end result is so much more than just preservation. The process of fermentation begins breaking down food, making the end product more easily digestible by the human body. This can provide relief to a system feeling the effects of modern processed foods, and can help balance the body to allow for healthy digestion and better absorption of nutrients.

Today in the United States, we are becoming aware of the health benefits of fermented foods. According to Tufts University's Gerald J. and Dorothy R. Friedman School of Nutrition Science and Food Policy, the fermentation process used to make sauerkraut and kimchi increases the glucosinolate in cabbage—naturally pungent compounds thought to fight cancer. Additionally, the healthy bacteria found in a number of fermented foods have been shown to increase immunity and decrease inflammation, autoimmune disorders, and allergies.

Supermarket shelves are lined with processed foods, such as breads, cheeses, vinegars, and condiments, all of which are laden with preservatives to keep them fresh. Additionally, many commercially packaged products undergo pasteurization to kill harmful bacteria, but this process also kills the healthy organisms your body needs. Although it may seem safer to eat these mass-produced products than items that you ferment in your own kitchen, that's just not true.

Traditionally, the acid in fermented foods serves as a natural, healthy preservative, eliminating the need for additional preservatives to extend shelf life. You can use this time-tested technique to take control of your food and preserve it in the most natural way possible. By fermenting in small batches, you can eat these healthy foods once you make them and refrigerate the leftovers, making heat processing unnecessary. Your body benefits when you eat the living, healthy bacteria produced through this simple method.

With only a few supplies, you can make a feast of fermented goodies at home, ranging from fermented berries to cream cheese to Indian naan bread. And once you master the basics, you can try your hand at some of the more time-consuming yet equally rewarding fermented foods, such as Cabernet Sauvignon, mead, miso paste, and soy sauce. This book is your trusty companion on your fermenting journey. On this trip we will explore classic and well-known fermentations, such as pickles, sauerkraut, kimchi, breads, and grains, as well as lesser-known ones, such as meats, fish, and legumes.

Each chapter is organized from beginner to advanced, helping you build on your fermentation skills from project to project. Although fermentation is often an unpredictable path, that shouldn't intimidate you. People around the world have been fermenting food for centuries, sometimes under less-than-hygienic conditions. If you follow the directions in this book and practice basic sanitation as you go along, you are all but guaranteed success.

These are approachable recipes for the home cook, and very few require fancy equipment—just items that are already in a well-stocked kitchen. Getting started with fermentation can be an interesting transition: Your kitchen may take on some unfamiliar aromas. The soured smell of sauerkraut, kimchi, or kombucha may be an unwelcome one at first. But as long as there are no signs of spoilage (as outlined in chapter 2, page 24), you are encouraged to finish the fermented food and try your results. You might not love everything on first bite, but as with many things in life, the amazing flavors and textures that fermentation produces will grow on you.

Are you already well versed in the nitty-gritty of fermentation? If so, there is no need to start with the basics. But reviewing them can improve your knowledge and ensure that you have the confidence to tackle some of the bigger projects in this book. Find your favorite fermented food, get started down a road of do-it-yourself fun, and enjoy the journey as you learn this ancient form of preservation.

FUNDAMENTALS I

1
THE BASICS

WHY FERMENT?

First and foremost, you should ferment because you enjoy the flavor of the end product. Whatever the health benefits, if you are going to keep up this practice, the results have to taste good, too. And the truth is that once you taste homemade cheeses, wines, yogurt, pickles, and other fermented foods, you may find that you never want to go back to their overly processed counterparts.

Fermentation, although most notable for providing a soured, complex taste to foods, also has other, more far-reaching implications. Packed with living bacteria, fermented foods can help increase overall health by providing probiotics to the gut. *Probiotics*, a term derived from the Greek prefix *pro-* and the Greek word *biota*, meaning "for life," are beneficial microorganisms found in the intestinal tracts of healthy individuals.

When these microorganisms are part of a healthy diet, they can help enhance the immune system, better synthesize nutrients from the food that is eaten, reduce symptoms of food allergies and intolerance, improve overall intestinal tract health, and reduce the risk of certain types of cancers. Regular consumption of these powerful living foods can provide an inexpensive, safe, and natural way to maintain health.

Fermenting foods can drastically extend the shelf life of foods. During the process of fermentation, the naturally occurring sugars in foods are broken down into acids, gas, or alcohol, which work as natural preservatives. Whether you are purchasing foods for fermentation from a market or growing them yourself, this method allows for much longer storage than when the foods are fresh, allowing you to eat all of your food without running the risk of spoilage.

And although sauerkraut or sourdough bread or pickles may cost a pretty penny at the farmers' market, you can make all of these products at home on the cheap. Use your own two hands to create amazingly delicious fermented foods for a fraction of what you would otherwise pay.

When you are first starting to add fermented foods to your diet, keep in mind that more is not always better. Because they are packed with bacteria, overconsumption can lead to adverse reactions in the digestive system. Instead, work to incorporate a variety of fermented foods into your diet over time. If you do not currently eat any raw, fermented foods, two tablespoons a day is enough to start. After your body is acclimated, the amount can be increased to a level that you are comfortable with and makes you feel good.

Although raw food ferments, such as sauerkraut, kimchi, and pickles, have living bacteria present, cooked fermented foods do not. These include sourdough bread, fermented grains, fermented legumes, and any other fermented food cooked at a temperature greater than 100°F. But a lack of beneficial bacteria does not mean that they should be excluded from the diet. Not all food we eat has to be probiotic—some can just taste great. Creating a balance between the two types of fermented foods is the best way to add value to your diet using this time-honored practice.

FERMENTING VS. PICKLING: WHAT'S THE DIFFERENCE?

Not all fermented items are pickled, and not all pickled items are fermented. Many people use the two terms interchangeably, but technically they are not the same. There are two different types of pickled foods—fresh and fermented. Fresh pickles use vinegar to achieve a soured taste, while fermented pickles are soured through the production of lactic acid.

Although vegetable or fruit pickles made through fermentation can be called pickled, foods made through pickling are not always fermented. Likewise, many fermented foods are pickled, but not all are—think sourdough bread or tofu. The rule of thumb is that if the item in question is made using vinegar as the souring medium, it is considered pickled and not fermented.

TYPES OF FERMENTATION

There are two basic types of fermentation: wild fermentation and starter fermentation. Wild fermentation relies on existing bacteria, yeasts, and mold in the environment to begin the process of fermentation. Starter fermentation requires the introduction of bacteria, yeast, or mold into a food to begin fermentation.

WILD FERMENTATION

Wild fermentation, as its name indicates, does not require any additional cultures or yeast. This is one of the leading methods used to make fermented vegetables, such as sauerkraut, pickles, or kimchi. Wild fermentation can also be used to make sourdough bread and to produce alcohol. A simple process, wild fermented foods use bacteria and yeasts in the air to transform foods into mouth-puckering, singularly soured masterpieces in the case of lacto-fermentation and acetic acid fermentation, and alcohol in the case of ethanol fermentation. By the time fermentation is complete, enough lactic acid, acetic acid, or alcohol has been produced that these products cannot be inhabited by harmful bacteria.

STARTER FERMENTATION

For many types of fermented foods, a starter is needed to introduce the proper bacteria, yeast, or mold necessary to create the desired finished product. Dairy fermented foods, such as yogurt and kefir, require a starter, as do beer, wine, kombucha, and cheese. The starter culture can take many forms, such as yeast in the case of wine or beer, a SCOBY (see page 14) for kombucha, or a do-it-yourself wild fermentation starter for sourdough breads. Many recipes that call for a starter culture require a specific type of culture for each different kind of food, while other recipes, such as those for cultured vegetables, can use a variety of starters to instigate the fermentation process. In many cases, the starter cultures can be reused for multiple batches, or they can consistently be taken from a new batch of the food or drink to continue making more in the future.

FERMENTATION METHODS

There are several methods used to ferment foods, and opinions vary as to which is the best. Salt, whey starter culture, and other starter cultures are among the most popular methods used for fruits, vegetables, meats, fish, grains, and seeds, and each has its own benefits and limitations. Based on the type of fermented food being made, as well as dietary factors, the following items can be employed to get the process started.

SALT

Salting food is the most time-honored method of fermentation. Salt, a desiccant (drying agent), works in the fermentation process by pulling moisture away from the food, thus preventing the growth of bacteria. Lactobacilli bacteria strains, which are the type that produce lactic acid, are salt-tolerant and thrive in these conditions, while mold and other bacteria strains are inhibited. Salt can also help keep vegetables crunchy during the fermentation process, an integral attribute of certain foods, such as cucumber pickles. Although the decomposition process will proceed without the use of salt, the salt prevents the wrong microorganisms from growing in the pickled food, and thereby prevents the putrefaction and off-flavors that would accompany an uncontrolled fermentation. The more salt used, the slower the fermentation.

DRY SALTING Dry salting is a method used to draw water from vegetables, fish, meats, or dairy. Sauerkraut is the most well-known fermented food that uses this method, but it is also widely used in cheese making and to cure meat and fish. When salt is added to the shredded cabbage that is the base for sauerkraut, over the course of 12 to 24 hours, the cabbage will release so much water that a brine will develop and cover the cabbage, allowing the fermentation process to begin. When dry salting is used with cheese, fish, or meat, the salt helps form a protective coating around the food to begin the preservation process.

BRINING Brining is a process in which water, salt, and other spices are combined to create a liquid that food is submerged in for fermentation. This process is often used when making cucumber pickles, as well as many other types of fermented vegetables. Once immersed in the brine, cucumbers begin to ferment, using either the wild yeasts and bacteria that are in the environment or a starter culture added to the brine. In some cases, both dry salting and brining are used in the same recipe.

STARTER CULTURES

WHEY Whey, a by-product of cheese making, is the liquid left over after the milk solids have been strained out or curdled. Whey is typically used together with salt to add flavor, as well as keep vegetable ferments crunchy. It is also popular in fruit fermented foods, in which the inherently salty flavor of a brine alone may not be enticing. Whey can be strained from cultured dairy products, such as yogurt, buttermilk, and kefir, and stored separately in the refrigerator until needed. Because whey contains lactose

(although the amount is minimal), it may not be a good choice for people who are lactose intolerant.

DRIED STARTER CULTURE Many types of packaged starter cultures are available to help take the guesswork out of fermenting. These contain different strains of dried bacteria and work in the same manner as whey to jump-start fermentation while providing some protection from undesirable bacteria growth. Commercial starter cultures are a necessary component of cheese making. There are also several varieties of vegetable and fruit fermenting starter cultures available that can be used in fermentation. When using a commercial starter culture, follow the instructions on the package for best results.

OTHER FERMENTING LIQUIDS Brine from other ferments, kombucha, or water kefir can be used as a starter culture for fermented fruits and vegetables. When making these substitutions, use 1/4 cup of the brine, kombucha, or water kefir for every quart of water to create an acid balance that protects foods from undesirable microbial growth.

OTHER FERMENTATION METHODS

SCOBY SCOBY, or a symbiotic culture of bacteria and yeast, is a starter specific to kombucha making. This gelatinous, bloblike culture feeds on the sugar in sweetened tea, transforming the tea into kombucha. SCOBYs can be purchased dried (these will need to be rehydrated), or they can be obtained from someone who regularly makes the beverage. Because the

SCOBY

Kefir grains

SCOBY increases in size and must be separated regularly during the process, people who make kombucha are often more than willing to give away a spare SCOBY.

KEFIR GRAINS Divided into two types, milk kefir grains and water kefir grains, these are packaged grains containing yeast and bacteria designed to make kefir, a type of cultured milk. Both types of grains require several days of rehydration before use. But once the kefir grains get going, and when they are well taken care of, they can continuously produce kefir for long periods before needing replacement.

YEAST Yeast is most often used to ferment alcoholic beverages. Although some types of beverages can employ wild yeast to get the job done, yeast is often recommended in order to prevent spoilage and maintain control over a fermenting alcoholic beverage. The type of yeast used for alcoholic fermentations is not the same as baking yeast. Beer and wine making use different strains of *Saccharomyces cerevisiae,* according to the type of beer or wine desired. Due to the ability of these cultivated yeast strains to create high alcohol levels without dying off, these yeasts are typically preferred to wild fermentation in beer and wine making.

SPROUTING Sprouting is used to prepare grains, seeds, and legumes immediately before consumption to increase their nutritional value. This ancient practice changes the composition of these foods, producing vitamin C, as well as increasing the vitamin B content. The process also neutralizes phytic acid, found in grains, which can prevent the absorption of magnesium, calcium, zinc, and iron in these foods. Sprouting also produces a variety of enzymes that add benefit during the digestion process, and neutralizes enzyme inhibitors that would prevent proper digestion of the carbohydrates in these foods.

SOAKING Unlike grains, seeds, and legumes, nuts cannot be sprouted. Instead, tree nuts, such as pine nuts, cashews, pecans, walnuts, almonds, and hazelnuts, can be soaked to break down enzyme inhibitors and allow the nuts to be more easily digested. This process entails submerging the nuts in saltwater overnight for harder nuts, such as almonds, or as little as four hours for smaller, softer nuts, such as pine nuts. By soaking the nuts before eating, their nutrients become more easily accessible to the body, and they are less likely to cause digestive distress. Once soaked, the nuts are then dried in a dehydrator, oven, or skillet again before eating.

HEALTH BENEFITS OF FERMENTING

Now that the history and basics are covered, we can get to the most interesting part of fermentation: it actually makes your food better for you. This simple process can improve the healthfulness of your food, making it more easily digestible and loaded with vitamins and enzymes.

EASY ON DIGESTION

Because fermented foods are already partially broken down through the process of fermentation, there is less work for your body to do to process them. In some cases, this allows people who are otherwise intolerant of certain foods, such as dairy or wheat, to eat foods that have been fermented with few or no side effects. Over time, eating fermented foods regularly can help improve digestion.

IMPROVES GUT FLORA

Optimal digestion requires a balance of healthy bacteria in the digestive tract. Regularly eating raw, fermented foods can provide this balance and help improve many chronic conditions, such as constipation, food intolerances, and allergies, by working from the inside out.

INCREASES ENZYMES

Enzymes help the body digest and get the most nutrition out of the food you eat every day. Without the proper enzymes, digestion can become sluggish and food will not be fully absorbed. Raw, fermented foods are loaded with the kinds of enzymes needed for healthy digestion, and the process of fermentation deactivates enzyme inhibitors that would otherwise prevent the seamless digestion and subsequent absorption of nutrients.

VITAMIN BOOST

Many foods actually have higher levels of vitamins when fermented than in their original state. Kimchi made from cabbage has higher levels of B vitamins than before fermentation. Kefir has higher levels of folic acid than milk, the product from which it's made. And even when the amount is not increased, in most cases, the vitamin content stays the same as before fermentation—something that cannot be said about cooked vegetables.

FROM THE MASTERS

CHONG CHOI, CO-FOUNDER AND HEAD OF PRODUCTION, CHOI'S KIMCHI COMPANY
www.choiskimchi.com

Back in Korea, it was customary for the women of the family to participate in making kimchi for the whole family. My siblings really had no interest when my grandmother would make it, but I would help when I could. I guess I had a curiosity about making kimchi at a very young age. Professionally, I thought I could produce a more quality kimchi than those that were readily available in stores, and my son Matt and I started Choi's Kimchi Company.

Early on, we thought it wise to have pathological testing completed on our product line. The laboratory instructed us to bring in our product as soon as production was over, before fermentation. They were not familiar with what kimchi was, and we had explained that it wasn't truly a finished product until fermentation was complete, but they went ahead and tested it anyway. They were alarmed by the results. They said that coliform levels were high, which was a cause of concern. I told them to settle down and keep testing every three days or so. Three days later

they called me back even more alarmed. Coliform levels had dropped off completely, and Lactobacillus was spiking. Fortunately, they were at ease after the next test, and we had a clean screening for our whole product line, but it goes to show you just how much transpires during the fermentation process.

They have a saying in Korea that translates roughly to "kimchi is a mystery" and it's something that I've personally experienced through the decades I've made kimchi. Don't be discouraged by a bad batch. Temperature, time, and salt content are among the most important factors to the end product of your kimchi. It's helpful to think of them as levers and knobs that can be varied to different results.

My favorite thing about kimchi is that there's not one way to make a good batch. Almost every cookbook, recipe, or author I've read on the subject has a different take on what's most important. I like that there's not one hard and fast formula.

2

IN THE KITCHEN

EQUIPMENT OVERVIEW

Don't be fooled by books or companies that propose you buy high-cost fermenting tools and accessories to get started. Fermenting is a project that can be tackled in your kitchen with just a clean work area, some jars, and a bit of refrigerator space. By starting simple, you gain confidence and learn the basics before you consider purchasing any specialized equipment for larger, more involved projects. Start with small batches so you can easily assess which projects you like best. This will also save you from having to devote a lot of refrigerator space to storing ferments.

FERMENTATION VESSELS

When you are starting out, you can ferment foods using readily available equipment. For fruits and vegetables, the easiest solution is to use glass mason jars. Pint, quart, and half-gallon mason canning jars are the least expensive way to ferment. That said, any large glass jar that is free of chips or cracks, and has a lid, will work just fine. These jars can also be used to sprout or soak grains, nuts, or seeds. Gather a mix of different sizes so that you can have several ferments going at once.

Various types of fermentation vessels are used for different projects, and these are outlined in each chapter as necessary. Specially designed fermentation jars fitted with air locks can be used for fruits or vegetables, and these are great for providing an anaerobic environment. They are not, however, truly necessary to get started. Once you get into wine and other fermented beverages, specialized fermentation vessels, such as carboys, are necessary, as well as air locks. But for most recipes in this book, you can choose your vessel based on your own preferences and budget.

You don't want to use any reactive metals (for example, aluminum, copper, iron, or steel) for fermentation. Reactive metals are great at conducting heat when cooking, but they are not appropriate for cooking or fermenting acidic or alkaline foods. Not only can these types of containers create metallic off-flavors in fermented foods, but some of the metal can actually leach into the finished ferment and ultimately cause harm to the body. Other materials, such as food-grade plastic or clay containers, can be used for fermentation. The liner of a slow cooker is a practical fermentation vessel that can be used for a slightly larger batch. But if you find yourself making a few larger batches a year, you may want to invest in a stoneware crock. Available in a range of sizes, from 1- to 10-gallon crocks, these are a durable investment.

UTENSILS, TOOLS, AND BASIC KITCHEN EQUIPMENT

Silicone or rubber spatulas are a necessity for mixing and stirring ferments. Although wooden spoons or wood handles work in the kitchen for other projects, they should be avoided for fermenting, as they can harbor unfriendly bacteria. A standard potato masher is also necessary to release the juices from various foods. A couple of good funnels (preferably one with a wide mouth and one with a narrow mouth) to fill jars and bottles make the process of storing your ferments mess-free.

Other tools, such as kitchen scissors, mesh strainers, and an instant-read kitchen thermometer, are also needed, as are a ladle, spoon, and slotted spoon made of stainless steel or other nonreactive metal. A mandoline to thinly slice vegetables makes many projects easier, but is not necessary when getting started. A solid, sharp kitchen knife, however, is a must for many projects.

A kitchen scale is vital to measure much of the produce in this book, but if you do not own one, measure produce at the store prior to purchase. Mixing bowls made of glass, ceramic, food-grade plastic, or stainless steel are necessary for many of the recipes here in order to evenly mix ingredients before packing them into a vessel. Nonreactive pots in a variety of sizes are also needed for cooking.

STORAGE

Once your ferments are complete, you will need bottles, jars, and containers in which to store the finished products. BPA-free plastic storage containers with lids in a variety of sizes are a great place to start. Glass jars, such as those in which the ferment was originally made, can easily be transferred to cold storage. Nonreactive lids are also good to have for acidic ferments, and can be purchased at most places that sell canning jars.

Swing-top beer bottles, such as the ones that Grolsch beer is sold in, are the best way to store many different types of beverages, and can withstand the pressure buildup in carbonated beverages. These can also be purchased new from home brewing shops. For still alcohol ferments, such as wine and mead, standard wine bottles are suitable. See our Resources section (page 193) to find out where to purchase these supplies.

Fermentation equipment (clockwise from top left): Mason Jar with lid, Potato masher, Funnel (small and large), Mesh strainer, Thermometer, Mixing Bowls (small and large), Digital kitchen scale, Chef's knife, Jar with airlock.

WEIGHTS

Many projects require a weight of some type to submerge foods in their brine for anaerobic fermentation. A variety of items can be used to weigh down food, depending on the fermentation vessel. For larger containers, a small plate or cleaned and sanitized rock will do the trick. For smaller containers, cleaned and sanitized glass coasters, glass votive candle holders, or glass shot glasses work well. Food-safe plastic storage bags filled with brine can be used to hold foods below the liquid's surface, and glass weights specifically designed for this purpose are sold by Pickle-It for use with their jars.

ESSENTIAL INGREDIENTS

Using the correct ingredients is absolutely essential when fermenting foods. Not only do the ingredients play a role in the flavor of the finished products, they can also help prevent spoilage. Although it may be possible to swap out ingredients, use the specific ingredients called for in a recipe.

SALT

Salt is an important element of fermenting. And not all salt is created equal, as most table salt has additives that prevent clumping. When this type of salt is added to a ferment, the result is a cloudy, hazy brine, which can make the food look unappetizing. Instead, choose pickling and canning salt or kosher salt. Sea salt can also be used, but avoid using any salt that is not white,

unless specifically called for in a recipe. In some cases, when using kosher salt, which has a large grain size, you may need to heat the liquid to enable it to dissolve fully. If this is the case, be sure to bring the brine back to room temperature before proceeding with the recipe.

WATER

If your water tastes and smells good, it probably is suitable for the projects in this book. If not, choose filtered water. Many municipal water systems add chlorine and fluoride to the water supply to protect the water from contamination. But chlorine can prevent the growth of the bacteria, yeast, and molds that are necessary for fermentation. Chlorine can be vaporized from water by boiling the water for two minutes. Let the water sit overnight before using it.

If you have hard water—hard enough that it discolors your bathtub and toilet with iron deposits—this will also translate to discolored pickles. Hard water can be boiled and then used after it has been left to sit for 24 hours. Ladle the water from the surface to avoid any sediment from the bottom of the pot.

WHEY

Whey can be obtained by straining homemade yogurt. Pour the yogurt into a fine mesh strainer lined with cheesecloth placed over a bowl. Once the whey has separated from the yogurt, which can take several hours, it can be stored by itself in the refrigerator in an airtight container for up to six months.

STARTER CULTURES

Starter cultures are important to introduce specific types of bacteria into a ferment. It is imperative that you select the correct culture for a specific project to ensure good results. Refer to Resources (page 193) for information on where to obtain starter cultures for particular projects.

APPLE CIDER VINEGAR

Apple cider vinegar is used in many of these recipes, but this is not conventional apple cider vinegar, which is pasteurized and filtered. Instead, use raw apple cider vinegar. Containing the "mother," a gelatinous blob composed of acetic acid bacteria that is responsible for turning the cider into vinegar, raw apple cider vinegar is teeming with beneficial bacteria to get a ferment going. Choose Bragg's brand or make your own from any apple variety (page 141).

HONEY

Raw, unfiltered honey is necessary for fermentation projects. Avoid commercially produced honey, because it is pasteurized and so will not contain the necessary bacteria to encourage fermentation. Raw honey is available seasonally from many farm stands and farmers' markets. Stock up when it is available, as honey has an indefinite shelf life.

HOW TO SELECT INGREDIENTS

Only the freshest ingredients should be used for fermenting. Organic, local produce is ideal. The most cost-effective way to ferment is to go with the seasons, selecting produce when it is readily available and at its lowest price. Knowing where your produce comes from can help you gauge its freshness. Getting to know farmers or employees at your local farmers' market or farm stand can also help you plan ahead, as you will know what is coming next and be ready for fermentation projects when they become available.

Don't be afraid to ask how old certain items are, as most farmers are upfront about their produce. They know that three-day old pickling cucumbers will produce a poor quality product and won't want to steer you down the wrong path. Although some ferments require the freshest of fresh produce, others, such as sauerkraut, can turn a cold-stored cabbage into a masterpiece. Either way, talk to the people who work at your local farmers' market or farm stand, and ask them plenty of questions.

When you choose fresh, sustainable, ethically raised, and antibiotic-free meats and fish, you are making the best choice, both for your body and for the environment. Frozen meats and fish that do not fulfill these standards are not ideal, but they can also be used for fermenting.

SUGAR

When sugar is called for in a recipe, choose unrefined cane sugar for the best results. Made from evaporated cane juice, this is the optimal choice for fermenting.

BASIC TROUBLESHOOTING

Although fermentation is not an exact science, there are many clues you can use as a guide to the success of your undertaking. As when you prepare other foods, your senses of smell, sight, and taste are the best guides to the progress of your project. For specific ferments, there are particular signs of spoilage or other problems, but the following simple, low-tech troubleshooting methods are a place to start for all of your different ferments. For information specific to a particular fermented food, see its associated chapter.

WHAT YOU SEE

When fermentation is under way, you will see tiny bubbles on the surface of your ferment. This is the simplest way to judge whether the process is taking place. When fermentation is in full swing, the bubbles will become more vigorous than at the beginning or end of fermentation, and can be used as a gauge to the development of the final product.

If any scum appears on the surface, it should be skimmed off immediately with a nonreactive utensil. Probably one of the most daunting aspects of fermenting is this matter of scum. Although unsightly, the scum is not harmful. If left in place, however, it can lead to spoilage, so care should be taken to remove it daily.

As fermentation progresses, the food may swell and expand. This is normal and not a sign of a problem. It is important to keep the fermenting food submerged in its liquid, and it should be regularly checked to ensure that the food is below the surface. If not, press it down again using weights. Keeping your fermenting items on a shelf or kitchen counter, where you can see them several times a day, means you can continually gauge progress and see right away if a problem occurs.

The color of a fermenting food may become dull, or the fermenting food may change color. This is an action of the enzymes in the food. The texture of the fermented food may change as well. This action is most noticeable in sauerkraut—the cabbage becomes the color of straw and pliable over the course of weeks. This is a sign that fermentation is taking place, not a sign of spoilage.

WHAT YOU SMELL

Fermenting food can have many different odors that may be new to you. But fermenting food should not smell putrid or rotting. If this occurs, dispose of the food without tasting it.

WHAT YOU TASTE

Fermented foods should taste good. If something does not taste good, toss it and try again. Be sure to clean fermenting vessels well, especially if signs of spoilage are present, to prevent recontamination.

FROM THE MASTERS

MICHELLE MITCHELL, CO-FOUNDER AND CHIEF CULTURAL ANGEL, HUMM KOMBUCHA
www.hummkombucha.com

Jamie Danek and I started Humm Kombucha in the winter of 2009. The stock market had crashed, every other house seemed to be for sale, and people were bumming. Yet in the midst of the chaos surrounding us, we were so happy. Jamie thought it was the kombucha; I was sure it had everything to do with the energy flowing through the drink. We felt so strongly about sharing the source of our happiness with others that we knew we had to expand our kombucha production. We started going door-to-door in the Prius, leaving full gallons of kombucha on people's porches. They left their empty gallons and $20 under the mat. And we had the most fun ever!

I just know that it's my mission in this lifetime to spread love and light throughout the world. It happens to be in a bottle of kombucha right now, in a live vessel that holds energy so clearly. Yet at the end of the day, it has everything to do with the joy that comes from the people who fill the brewery, and capture some of it in every bottle. It's an honor for us to be in this time and space with other kombucha brewers, educating the public on the health benefits of this age-old drink. We're all in this together, and the more people who brew and serve their drink to others, the healthier we all are as a collective community!

FERMENTING ENVIRONMENT

One of the biggest factors that can contribute to the success or failure of a fermentation project is its environment. Most fermented foods require very specific environments, which are for the most part easily maintainable in a typical home. However, failure to adhere to these guidelines can result in a fermentation that does not achieve its potential or one that becomes spoiled.

TEMPERATURE

Fermented foods must be kept at a steady temperature throughout the process. Fluctuations greater than five degrees should be avoided. Try to find an area in your kitchen that can maintain a room temperature between 68°F and 72°F for best results and flavor. The higher the temperature, the quicker the fermentation, and fermentation times directly relate to the end flavor of the food. Keep in mind the seasonal fluctuations in your home's temperature and adjust accordingly. In the heat of the summer, you may need to move your ferments to a cooler location to slow down the process. For meats, humidity must also be maintained and monitored.

SUNLIGHT

Fermented food should be kept away from direct sunlight during fermentation. This prevents changes in temperature that can affect the quality of the food. A dark cupboard is a good place to ferment small batches of food, but only if you are disciplined enough to remember your food when it is hidden behind closed doors. A forgotten ferment can lead to a messy cleanup later.

FINISHED FERMENTS

Different ferments benefit from different storage conditions. As a general rule, however, most finished ferments can be stored in a home refrigerator with good results. Standard storage temperature for finished ferments is between 38°F and 50°F. This can also allow for storage in a cool basement, cellar, wine cooler, or other chilly area of your house. Fermented foods can be frozen for short periods, but after extended storage, the probiotic benefits of the food will be lost.

BASIC FERMENTATION TIMES AND TEMPERATURES

FERMENTED FOOD	TIME TO FERMENT	FERMENTING TEMPERATURE
Sauerkraut	5 to 6 weeks 2 to 3 weeks	60°F 70°F to 75°F
Kimchi	3 to 6 days	68°F
Cucumber Pickles	2 to 4 weeks	72°F
Other Fermented Vegetables	1 to 3 weeks	72°F
Fruit Ferments	12 to 48 hours	72°F
Kefir	12 to 24 hours	70°F to 77°F
Yogurt	12 to 18 hours	110°F to 115°F
Cultured Buttermilk, Sour Cream, Cultured Butter	12 to 24 hours	70°F to 77°F
Cream Cheese	12 hours	70°F to 77°F
Grains	12 to 36 hours	68°F to 72°F
Fermented and Sprouted Legumes	8 to 36 hours	68°F to 72°F
Natto (see p. 123)	8 hours	100°F
Miso and Soy Sauce	6 months to 1 year	68°F to 72°F
Tempeh	24 to 48 hours	85°F to 90°F
Fermented Miso	3 to 5 days	40°F
Fermented Grains	12 to 36 hours	68°F to 75°F
Fermented Meats	5 to 7 days	40°F
Fermented Fish	12 to 24 hours	68°F to 72°F
Vinegar	4 to 8 weeks	68°F to 72°F
Condiments	2 to 4 days	68°F to 72°F
Kombucha	7 to 10 days	72°F to 78°F
Water Kefir	2 to 4 days	68°F to 72°F
Kvass (see p. 162)	2 to 7 days	68°F to 72°F
Mead	4 weeks	70°F to 75°F
Hard Cider	2 to 3 weeks	70°F to 75°F
Wine	5 to 6 weeks 1 month or more for clearing	70°F to 75°F

FERMENTING BEST PRACTICES

Because you are working with living foods, you must take care to protect them from various elements that can harm them. By following these simple best practices, you can be sure that your ferments live a long, healthy life—all the way into your gut.

CLEANING AND SAFETY

Keeping your work space clean is an important aspect of success in fermentation. Use these tips as a guide to ensure your fermenting projects run smoothly from start to finish.

- Sanitize your work space before beginning a project by using distilled vinegar sprayed on a towel to get rid of any lingering harmful bacteria on your countertops.

- Wash and sanitize all utensils and equipment before beginning a project. Use warm, soapy water followed by a thorough rinse to clean equipment and utensils, and then submerge all items in a bleach-water solution. Rinse the items again and allow them to air-dry before using.

- Always wash your hands before beginning a project or checking on an active ferment. Unscented soap is ideal. Antibacterial soap should be avoided. Rinse your hands thoroughly and dry well before proceeding.

- Avoid cross contamination in the kitchen by working on only one project at a time. Wash and sanitize cutting boards between projects. Most fermentation projects are quick and straightforward, and focusing all your attention on one thing at a time prevents mistakes.

TRACKING YOUR PROJECTS

Take good notes throughout the course of each project. This allows you to get a sense of what works and what doesn't in your own environment. Review your notes before you get started on a new project to continue learning from both your major wins and your less-than-successful experiments.

RECIPES

II

3

VEGETABLES

Fermented vegetables have been around for centuries, accompanying humans on tasks both great and small. From their first recorded appearance at the building of the Great Wall of China, to a supporting role in the cuisine of ancient Rome, to their ubiquitous part in the diet of Europeans since the Middle Ages, fermented vegetables have secured an enduring place in human history.

More than a technique most likely developed as a way to stretch the harvest, fermentation is a way of life. It is a cyclical, time-honored art form that binds you to the land, the seasons, and the world around you. It is carried out in small houses in villages that lack electricity and in grand houses with all the latest accoutrements in major metropolitan areas. No matter your location or income, fermenting at home is a step you can take to control your food, improve your health, and create something special with your own two hands.

Along with facilitating digestion, vegetable fermentations can increase the vitamin levels in foods, while simultaneously creating some amazingly complex flavor combinations. Termed *lacto-fermentation*, or lactic acid fermentation, vegetable fermentations can run the gamut from crunchy to sweet to sour, and sometimes all three at once. Making use of the omnipresent lactobacilli bacteria found on all forms of produce, lacto-fermentation turns these bacteria into lactic acid, giving this category of ferments its distinctly sour flavor.

SPECIAL CONSIDERATIONS

Most of the recipes in this chapter call for pickling salt. It is a very fine grain, similar to table salt, and therefore it is easily dissolved in water. But if you can't find pickling salt at a store near you, another salt, such as kosher salt or pure sea salt, can be used. Because many of these salts have a coarse grain, you may need to heat the brine to dissolve them. If this is the case, be sure to bring the brine back to room temperature before continuing with the recipe, or hasten the process by dissolving the salt in a small amount of heated water and adding the remaining cool water to the pan to quickly cool the mixture.

Most of the recipes in this chapter can be made using 1- or 2-quart (half-gallon) mason jars. But they can all be multiplied or divided to suit your needs. Keep in mind that larger batches require larger or more fermentation vessels. There are many places to purchase reasonably priced fermentation crocks, or you can repurpose other items in your kitchen for fermentation. Gallon glass jars are great for pickles, while an enameled Dutch oven can work well to make a larger batch of sauerkraut or pickles. You can also divide a batch into several quart jars or half-gallon jars to make it fit in your refrigerator. Work with what you have, when possible, until your fermentation projects outgrow your kitchen's supplies.

Using organic produce is the best way to ensure that a fermented food gets off to a good start, with the necessary bacteria present to encourage its growth. Conventionally grown produce, meaning any produce that is grown with the use of synthetic chemicals, is often loaded with antibacterial, antimicrobial, and antifungal agents, which can interfere with fermentation. Organic produce, on the other hand, is loaded with beneficial bacteria, which is present in the atmosphere around us and which helps instigate fermentation. By creating the proper environment through the addition of salt or a starter culture, fermentation takes place largely on its own with little need for help from you. All produce should be rinsed and dried before use, with the exception of tightly leafed items, such as cabbage. In the case of these items, the outer leaves can be removed until the head is visibly clean.

WHAT TYPE OF CLOSURE SHOULD I USE?

There are three major types of closure. Although each closure has its benefits and drawbacks, any one of them will work for the recipes in this book. Choose whichever suits you best, or experiment with all three.

- Standard canning lids can be used, and because they come with the jars, they are often the easiest and most cost-effective solution. The one caveat is that you must "burp" the jar daily to prevent excessive gas buildup in the jar during active fermentation. If left unchecked for several days, excessive gas buildup could cause a jar to explode. Burp the jar by loosening the ring of the lid to allow the gas to escape—in most cases, you can hear the gas exiting the jar without removing the lid.

- A lid fitted with an air lock can help prevent food from becoming oxidized, as well as promote anaerobic fermentation—the type of fermentation that takes place without oxygen, which most of these recipes use. An air lock is a two- or three-piece tool made up of a body, piston, and vented cap. When filled with water and fitted into a drilled hole on the lid of a jar, the air lock allows for the release of built-up gas without allowing oxygen in. To use an air lock, you will need special fermenting jars that are fitted with drilled holes on the jar lid. For information on where to purchase these, see page (193) in the Resources section.

- A clean, zippered freezer bag filled with brine is also a functional way to both weight down a ferment and lock out oxygen. The bag is stuffed into the mouth of the jar, creating a barrier for oxygen. The brine is the same as the brine in the jar, so if the bag leaks or breaks, this does not pose a problem. Place a plate underneath the jar to catch dripping brine.

SAUERKRAUT

MAKES: 2 QUARTS **PREP TIME:** 20 MINUTES **FERMENTATION TIME:** 2 TO 6 WEEKS

BEGINNER

Sauerkraut is a cornerstone of fermenting, and it is surprisingly simple to make. Viewed as a health food for hundreds of years, sauerkraut was carried on European ships to prevent scurvy because of its high levels of vitamin C. It is a time-tested fermented food that can build your confidence for a number of other fermenting projects. This basic recipe creates a slightly sweet, complex sauerkraut that pairs well with grilled meats and sandwiches. This recipe can be easily scaled up by multiplying the ingredients. For best results, choose fresh-picked cabbage, which will release enough liquid after salting that the cabbage will be covered in its own brine. Cabbage that has been stored will also work, but additional brine may be needed to submerge the cabbage.

1 small head white cabbage (about 2 to 2½ pounds)
1 tablespoon juniper berries (optional)
1½ tablespoons pickling salt

1. Prepare the cabbage by first removing its hard inner core. Remove a couple of its outer leaves, reserving these for later. Split the cabbage into quarters, and thinly slice it using a sharp knife, or shred it on a mandoline. Whichever tool you use, cut the cabbage into shreds about ¼-inch thick (see fig. A).

2. Place the cabbage and the juniper berries (if using) in a large nonreactive bowl. Mix the salt together with the cabbage, massaging them with your bare, clean hands so that the salt is evenly mixed throughout the cabbage (see fig. B). Leave the salted shreds to sit for 5 to 10 minutes, or until the cabbage begins to release some juices.

3. Once the cabbage begins to soften and a small amount of juice has gathered at the bottom of the bowl, pack the contents of the bowl into a half-gallon jar or two quart jars. Using a clean fist or a smaller jar, pound the cabbage down firmly to fit all of it into the jar(s) (see fig. C).

On top of the salted cabbage, place one or two reserved leaves to hold it down and form a barrier. Weigh the cabbage down using a glass weight, clean stone, or other nonreactive weight. At this point, the cabbage may not be fully immersed in brine. To accelerate the release of brine, add another heavy weight. Fill a narrow-mouth 8-ounce or 10-ounce jelly jar with water, cap it, and insert it into the opening of the jar over the weight to apply more pressure. Alternatively, fill a food-safe zippered bag with 1½ tablespoons pickling salt and 4 cups water,

and insert this bag into the opening of the jar. Cover the entire jar with a clean kitchen towel, and leave out at room temperature (see fig. D).

4. Within 24 hours, the cabbage should release enough liquid that the cabbage is covered in its own brine. If the amount of brine is inadequate, a brine can be made using 1½ tablespoons pickling salt and 4 cups water. Use this as needed to cover the cabbage. The cabbage should remain below the surface of the brine at all times. Weight the cabbage down again. Cover the jar using a clean, tightly woven dishtowel. Place the jar in a cool location away from direct sunlight.

5. Check the cabbage daily and if any scum appears on the surface, skim it off immediately with a nonreactive utensil. Rinse off the weights, as well, when scum appears.

6. After 2 weeks, begin checking the sauerkraut for taste. Because sauerkraut fermentation is highly variable based on temperature, it can take 2 to 6 weeks to be complete. When fermented at 70°F to 75°F, the sauerkraut will take 2 to 3 weeks. When fermented at 60°F, the sauerkraut can take 5 to 6 weeks. The best indication that fermentation is complete is that bubbles stop rising to the surface.

7. Once the sauerkraut is fermented to your liking, place a lid on the jar and close it tightly. Store the jar in your refrigerator until you are ready to use its contents.

A CLOSER LOOK

Sauerkraut is typically made in the fall, when cabbage is fresh and temperatures begin to drop. Cooler temperatures during fermentation produce a sauerkraut that is more complex in flavor, as well as one with higher levels of vitamin C. During hotter months, an air-conditioned room, basement, or other cool place can help you create delicious masterpieces year-round.

SAUERKRAUT TROUBLESHOOTING TIPS

PROBLEM	POTENTIAL CAUSE
Mold on top	Too high a temperature during fermentation or fermentation vessel not properly covered. Remove moldy sauerkraut and proceed.
Dark color at top	High fermentation temperatures and uneven salting cause oxidation. Remove the darkened portion from container and proceed.
Pink sauerkraut	Caused by yeast growth due to uneven salting, inadequate use of weights to hold cabbage below brine, or excessive salting. Remove pink sauerkraut and proceed.
Scum on top	Caused by yeast growth. Work to better exclude air and keep cabbage below the brine. Skim the scum daily with a nonreactive utensil.
Sliminess	An indication of spoilage. Caused by too high a temperature during fermentation, or by using too little salt. Discard the sauerkraut.

WINE SAUERKRAUT

WEINSAUERKRAUT

MAKES: 2 QUARTS **PREP TIME:** 20 MINUTES **FERMENTATION TIME:** 2 TO 6 WEEKS

BEGINNER

A standard throughout Germany, *weinsauerkraut* has yet to hit the mainstream in the United States. Using a dry white wine in the brine takes sauerkraut and transforms it into something extraordinary with a subtle yet bright flavor all its own. Like other sauerkraut recipes, this can easily be multiplied or divided to create a larger or smaller batch. With a taste profile that stands out from the typical sauerkraut, wine kraut pairs exceptionally well with hearty sausage for a German-style meal.

1 small head green cabbage (about 2 to 2½ pounds)

1½ tablespoons pickling salt

¼ cup dry white wine

1. Prepare the cabbage by first removing its hard inner core. Remove a couple of its outer leaves, and reserve these for later. Split the cabbage into quarters, and thinly slice it using a sharp knife, or shred it on a mandoline. Whichever tool you choose, cut the cabbage into thin shreds about ¼-inch thick.

2. Place the cabbage in a large bowl. Mix the salt together with the cabbage, massaging the ingredients with your clean bare hands so that the salt is evenly mixed throughout the leaves. Let the cabbage sit on the counter for 5 to 10 minutes, or until it begins to release a bit of its juice.

3. Pack the cabbage into a 2-quart jar. Using a clean fist, pound the cabbage down firmly to fit it all in the jar. Add one or two cabbage leaves to the top of the jar to cover the cabbage, tucking them down around the outside edges. Weigh the cabbage down using a glass weight, clean stone, or other nonreactive weight. To encourage the release of juice, place a narrow-mouth 8- or 10-ounce jelly jar filled with water on top of the weight. Alternatively, fill a food-safe zippered storage bag with ¾ tablespoon salt and 2 cups water, and place this into the mouth of the jar to weight down the cabbage. Cover the jar using a clean kitchen towel, and store it in a cool location.

4. Within 24 hours, remove the weights and add the wine. After the addition of the wine, the cabbage should be submerged in its brine. If not, a brine can be made using ¾ tablespoon salt dissolved in 2 cups water to cover the cabbage. The cabbage should remain below the surface of the brine at all times. Weight the cabbage down again. Cover the jar with a clean towel. Place the jar in a cool location.

5. Check the jar daily for the formation of scum on the surface. If it appears, skim the scum off with a nonreactive utensil and rinse the weights before replacing.

6. After 2 weeks, begin testing the sauerkraut. If it is soured and slightly softened to your liking, it can be moved into the refrigerator to slow fermentation. If you would prefer it a bit more soured, leave it to ferment longer. The fermentation process can take 2 to 6 weeks, depending on the temperature at fermentation. The best indication that fermentation is complete is that bubbles stop rising in the jar.

7. Once complete, remove the weights and cabbage leaves, and cap the jar tightly with a lid. Store the jar in the refrigerator.

TRY INSTEAD

Sauerkraut should be stored in a cold location, typically around 38°F. If you start making large batches of sauerkraut, space may become an issue. Sauerkraut can be canned; however, it loses much of its probiotic properties with heat processing. To can, pack the cold sauerkraut and its juices into 1-pint or 1-quart canning jars, leaving ½-inch headspace. Close the jars with two-piece tops, and process in a boiling water bath for 20 minutes (pints) or 25 minutes (quarts). Prevent breakage by ensuring that the water is not yet boiling when the cold jars are added to it.

CURTIDO

MAKES: 1 QUART **PREP TIME:** 15 MINUTES PREP TIME, 1 HOUR RESTING
FERMENTATION TIME: 2 DAYS

BEGINNER

The lightly fermented *curtido* hails from El Salvador and is similar to cole-slaw. Shredded cabbage, carrots, onions, and chiles come together to create the mildly spicy and distinctive flavor of this classic dish. Traditionally served alongside *pupusas* (thick corn tortillas stuffed with a variety of fillings), cur-tido can complement a range of flavors. Fermented for a couple of days—which is quick compared with the much longer time needed to create sauerkraut—curtido retains a crisp texture and crunchiness that set it apart from other cabbage-based concoctions.

1 small head cabbage (about 2 pounds)

2 carrots

½ red onion

4 green onions

Small handful cilantro

2 Serrano chiles, minced

1 teaspoon red pepper flakes

1 teaspoon pickling salt

¼ cup white wine vinegar

2 tablespoons pineapple juice

1. Prepare the cabbage by coring and shredding it by hand or in a food processor. Shred the carrots and red onion using a box grater or food processor. Cut the green onions into thin rounds. Mince the cilantro.

2. In a large bowl, mix the cabbage, carrots, red onion, green onion, and cilantro. Add the Serrano chiles, crushed red pepper, and salt, and continue to mix.

3. Leave the vegetables sitting at room temperature for about 1 hour, or until they release some liquid.

4. Pack the vegetables into a quart jar, and press them down with a clean hand to remove air pockets. Pour the brine from the bowl into the jar, and add the white wine vinegar and pineapple juice. Press the vegetables down so that they are completely covered by the brine.

5. Use a weight to hold the cabbage and other vegetables below the surface.

6. Place a lid loosely on the jar and leave it at room temperature for 2 days.

7. Close the lid tightly. Transfer the curtido to the refrigerator, where it can be stored for up to 3 weeks.

KIMCHI

With this simple recipe, kimchi can easily become a regular addition to your table. The benefit of making it yourself is that you are able to bend the recipe to suit your taste, adding or subtracting Korean ground hot pepper based on your desired heat level. As with other vegetable ferments, kimchi can be stored for long periods, so there is no need to make just a small batch if you have a lot of produce on hand. Kimchi uses a different process than sauerkraut, using a liquid brine in place of dry salting. Napa cabbage is the traditional main ingredient of this spicy and sour pickle, and in addition to being eaten by itself, it can be used to season soups and rice dishes.

1 small head napa cabbage (about 1½ pounds)

2 tablespoons plus ¾ teaspoon pickling salt

4 cups water

4 scallions, slivered

1 tablespoon minced ginger

1½ tablespoons Korean ground hot pepper

¾ teaspoon sugar

1. Trim the napa cabbage into 2-inch squares.

2. Dissolve the 2 tablespoons salt in the water. Pour the brine over the cabbage in a bowl or other fermenting vessel, and weight down the cabbage with a plate. Cover the bowl with a clean kitchen towel. Let the cabbage stand at room temperature for 12 hours.

3. Place a colander over a bowl and pour the cabbage into it to drain, reserving the brine. Add all the remaining ingredients, including the last ¾ teaspoon salt, to the cabbage, mixing it thoroughly to ensure everything is well incorporated.

4. Pack the cabbage mixture into a clean quart jar, pressing it down firmly as you proceed. Pour the brine over the cabbage until it is covered.

5. Use a weight to submerge the cabbage in the brine. Affix a lid or fill a food-safe zippered bag with any remaining brine, seal it, and pack it into the mouth of the jar to keep the cabbage below the surface.

Continued

6. Place the kimchi in a cool place, about 68°F, and allow it to ferment for 3 to 6 days. Taste the kimchi after 3 days, and continue to ferment it until it is to your liking.

7. Once complete, remove the brine bag or weight, cap the jar, and transfer it to your refrigerator, where the kimchi will keep for several months.

TRY INSTEAD

Dried Korean hot peppers are used generously in kimchi to give it a distinct color and mild heat. If you are unable to locate them, Mexican or New Mexican ground peppers, which are available in many grocery stores, are comparable. If you are unable to find any of these, paprika and cayenne can be mixed together in a ratio that suits your taste.

DAIKON AND CABBAGE KIMCHI

MAKES: 1 QUART **PREP TIME:** 15 MINUTES PREP TIME, 12 HOURS RESTING
FERMENTATION TIME: 3 TO 6 DAYS

BEGINNER

Daikon adds a complementary crunch to kimchi. Although plain cabbage kimchi is great because of its versatility, this radish-flecked version is best eaten straight and savored for its wonderfully firm texture. It pairs well with plenty of Asian-inspired meals, and can add a bit of welcome spice to your plate no matter what kind of cuisine you enjoy. If you are not a fan of spicy foods, cut back on the ground hot pepper to create a kimchi that is all your own and well suited to your palate.

½ small head napa cabbage (about ¾ pound)
¾ pound daikon radish
2 tablespoons pickling salt, divided
4 cups water
4 scallions, sliced
1 tablespoon ginger, minced
1 tablespoon Korean ground hot pepper
¾ teaspoon sugar

1. Prepare the cabbage by dicing it into 2-inch squares. Cut the daikon into thin rounds.

2. Dissolve 1 tablespoon and 2 teaspoons pickling salt in the water. Pour the brine, cabbage, and daikon into a large nonreactive bowl or fermenting vessel. Weight the cabbage and daikon down using a plate, and cover the bowl with a clean kitchen towel. Let stand for 12 hours.

3. Place a colander over a bowl, and pour the cabbage into it to drain, reserving the brine.

4. Mix all the remaining ingredients into the cabbage and daikon, including the remaining teaspoon pickling salt.

5. Pack the mixture into a quart jar. Pour the remaining brine into the jar to cover it. Weight down the cabbage and daikon, and affix a lid loosely on the jar. Alternatively, add the remaining brine to a food-safe zippered bag and seal the bag. Push the brine bag into the mouth of the jar, and place the jar in a cool location with a temperature of around 68°F.

6. Let the kimchi ferment for 3 to 6 days. Taste the ferment after the third day, and continue fermenting until it is as sour as you prefer.

7. Once complete, remove the brine bag or weight, cap the jar with a nonreactive top, and move the kimchi to the refrigerator, where it will keep for several months.

CABBAGE, APPLE, AND CARROT KIMCHI

MAKES: 1 QUART **PREP TIME:** 20 MINUTES PREP TIME, 4 TO 6 HOURS RESTING
FERMENTATION TIME: 3 TO 6 DAYS

BEGINNER

Carrot adds crunch and apple brings a hint of sweetness to this alternative kimchi, a tasty twist on tradition. There are as many ways to make kimchi as the imagination allows, and this is a Japanese-inspired one. This slightly sweet kimchi can be eaten along with rice for a light meal, or served as a snack along with beer.

1 small head Chinese cabbage (about 1½ pounds)
2 tablespoons plus 1 teaspoon pickling salt
2 carrots, grated
1 small crisp apple, grated
2 scallions, thinly sliced
1 teaspoon ginger, minced
1 garlic clove
¾ teaspoon Korean ground hot pepper
1 cup water

1. Cut the Chinese cabbage into 2-inch squares. Place the cabbage in a nonreactive bowl, and sprinkle it with 2 tablespoons of the pickling salt; mix well so that the pieces are evenly covered. Place a clean kitchen towel on top, and leave the mixture to sit at room temperature for several hours, until it is reduced in size by at least half. Drain the excess water from the bowl. Fill the bowl with water, and rinse the cabbage again, pressing it to remove as much water as possible.

2. Mix all the remaining ingredients, including the additional teaspoon salt. Pack into a quart jar, and top the jar with water.

3. Place a lid or a top with an air lock on the jar, and leave the jar in a cool area of your kitchen for 3 to 6 days. If using a standard top, loosen the cap daily after fermentation begins, to allow gas to escape.

4. Once the kimchi is fermented to your liking, cap the jar tightly and place it in cold storage, such as the refrigerator.

TRY INSTEAD

Although this recipe calls for apple, this type of kimchi is traditionally made using Japanese or Asian pear. Because these are not widely available in the United States, apple is the closest substitute. Asian pear, which crunches like an apple, is slightly sweet and sour, creating a rich flavor in any dish in which it is incorporated. If Japanese or Asian pears are available, use one of them instead in this recipe.

MIXED PICKLES

Cauliflower, carrots, and red peppers are complementary vegetables that come together to create this crisp pickle combination, teeming with both flavor and crunch. Perfect for a crudité platter, as an add-in for a pasta dish, or simply as a snack to munch on throughout the day, this tri-pickle mixture is sure to enthrall your taste buds. Start simple with this assortment of produce and spices, and once you've got the basic recipe down, experiment on your own with your preferred flavor combinations.

1 cup trimmed cauliflower florets

1 cup sliced carrots

1 cup sliced red bell pepper

3 shallots, sliced

2 garlic cloves, crushed

½ teaspoon coriander seeds

¼ teaspoon peppercorns

2 tablespoons pickling salt

2 cups water

2 teaspoons red wine vinegar

1. Layer the vegetables, shallots, garlic, and spices in the jar. Dissolve the salt in the water, and pour over the vegetables until covered. Add the red wine vinegar to the jar.

2. Use a weight to hold the vegetables below the brine.

3. Cap the jar using a standard lid, a lid with an air lock, or a freezer bag filled with brine. Keep the jar at room temperature.

4. Once bubbles begin forming, check the fermented food daily for scum. If any appears, skim it off immediately with a nonreactive utensil. If using a standard cap, unscrew it every day or two to allow built-up gas to escape.

5. Taste the fermented food after 2 to 3 weeks, when the bubbling has stopped. If the pickles are soured to your liking, cap the jar tightly and put the jar in cold storage, such as the refrigerator.

LACTO-FERMENTED GREEN BEANS

MAKES: 1 QUART **PREP TIME:** 15 MINUTES **FERMENTATION TIME:** 2 WEEKS

BEGINNER

Fermented green beans can provide some serious snap to a Bloody Mary, or can be eaten on their own as a side dish or snack. Although this recipe calls for staples such as garlic and dill, these beans can also be made to suit a variety of tastes by adding your favorite seasoning or herbs. Any herbs and spices can be swapped in or out at similar levels, but be sure to include the correct amount of salt to prevent spoilage.

½ pound tender snap beans, trimmed
2 garlic cloves, crushed
4 peppercorns, crushed
2 dill heads
2 tablespoons pickling salt
3 cups water

1. Layer the beans, garlic, peppercorns, and dill in a quart jar. Dissolve the salt in the water, and pour over the beans until covered. Cap the jar using a standard lid, a lid with an air lock, or a freezer bag filled with brine. Store at room temperature.

2. Fermentation should begin within 3 days and will be visible by the tiny bubbles rising in the jar. Once fermentation begins, check the jar daily for scum, and skim it off with a nonreactive utensil should it occur.

3. Fermentation will be complete in about 2 weeks, once bubbles cease to rise and the beans taste soured. Remove the weight or brine bag, cap the jar using a nonreactive top, and keep refrigerated.

LACTO-FERMENTED SALSA

MAKES: 1 QUART **PREP TIME:** 20 MINUTES **FERMENTATION TIME:** 2 DAYS

BEGINNER

Technically, tomatoes are a fruit. They are included here because in this recipe they are prepared in the manner of vegetable ferments. A starter culture is used to get the fermentation going, but salt is also included, as it provides flavor to the finished product. This fermented salsa will last longer in the refrigerator, and will be teeming with probiotics, which make it even healthier than fresh salsa!

3 cups chopped tomatoes
1 red onion, diced
4 garlic cloves, minced
¼ cup fresh cilantro, coarsely chopped
3 scallions, coarsely chopped
2 jalapeños, finely diced
2 tablespoons kosher salt
Juice of 1 lemon
Juice of 1 lime
½ cup whey (page 23)

1. Add the tomatoes, onion, garlic, cilantro, scallions, and jalapeños to a large nonreactive bowl and toss well. Add the salt and citrus juices. Mix well. Add the whey and mix again.

2. Pack the salsa into a 2-quart mason jar or glass fermenting jar with an air lock. Secure the lid. Leave on the counter at room temperature for 2 days.

3. Transfer the salsa to the refrigerator to store until ready to use. This recipe tastes best after a couple of weeks in the refrigerator.

TRY INSTEAD

If you prefer a green salsa, you can easily swap tomatillos for the tomatoes in this recipe. Use green salsa on tacos, enchiladas, or burritos in the same way as you would red salsa, or serve it alongside tortilla chips for an energizing snack.

LACTO-FERMENTED BEETS

MAKES: 1 QUART **PREP TIME**: 10 MINUTES **FERMENTATION TIME**: 3 TO 12 DAYS

BEGINNER

If you boil beets, then you actually throw out many of their nutrients with the cooking water. If you ferment them raw, you will not only take advantage of the full nutritional value of this sweet, earthy root vegetable, but you will gain the benefits of probiotics. Here, we recommend cutting the beets into matchsticks, but any cut will do, really—just keep in mind that larger cuts will require longer fermentation times.

3½ cups beets, cut into large matchsticks
2 tablespoons kosher or sea salt
2 cups water

1. Prepare the beets and pack them into a quart jar.

2. Mix the salt in the water until the salt is dissolved. Pour the brine over the beets. Weight the beets down so that they are totally submerged in the brine.

3. Secure the jar lid, and attach an air lock if available. If using a standard lid, unscrew the jar lid every couple of days to prevent too much gas from building up.

4. Begin tasting the beets after 3 days to gauge their sourness. Continue to ferment, checking daily, until they have reached the desired texture and flavor, and then transfer to cold storage.

PAIR IT

Think outside the box and use pickled beets as part of a veggie sandwich. Toast two slices of hearty bread, and build flavorful layers with feta cheese, pickled beets, and pesto—start with a few slices of feta on the bottom, add a heaping pile of drained pickled beets, and spread pesto on the top slice of bread for a filling and delicious vegetarian lunch.

LACTO-FERMENTED CARROT SPEARS

MAKES: 1 QUART PREP TIME: 15 MINUTES FERMENTATION TIME: 2 WEEKS

BEGINNER

For children, and even for many adults (let's be honest, here), eating the recommended daily dose of vegetables can be difficult. But this will not be the case when you have a fermented jar of carrots lying around. These slightly sweet carrots are a showstopper as a side dish, and possess a soured, garlicky tang that is quite habit-forming. Forget about telling your kids to eat all their vegetables when these are on the table—they will disappear before your eyes.

1 pound carrots
4 garlic cloves, peeled
2 tablespoons pickling salt
2 cups water

1. Cut the carrots into sticks by quartering them. For longer carrots, cut them in half again.

2. Place the garlic cloves at the bottom of the jar. Pack the carrots into the jar vertically, wedging them in tightly but not so tightly that the brine cannot circulate around them.

3. Mix the salt and water until the salt is dissolved. Pour the brine over the carrots. Use a weight to keep the carrots submerged.

4. Close the jar with either a lid or a lid with an air lock. If using a standard lid, be sure to open the jar slightly by unscrewing it every few days to allow gas to escape before resealing it.

5. Keep the jar at room temperature. After 7 days, begin tasting the fermented carrots. Once they are soured to your liking, which can take up to 2 weeks, place the cap on the jar tightly and transfer to cold storage.

TRY INSTEAD

This recipe is highly customizable to your tastes. A simple variation is to grate the carrots before fermenting and then use the final product to top a salad or pasta dish. Spices and herbs, such as dill, oregano, thyme, or ginger, can also work well with this vegetable. Add 1 or 2 pinches of dried herbs, a sprig of fresh, or a slice of ginger to your ferment and see what you think of the results.

ASIAN-STYLE FERMENTED DAIKON

MAKES: 1 QUART **PREP TIME:** 10 MINUTES **FERMENTATION TIME:** 2 TO 5 DAYS

BEGINNER

Daikon, a Japanese radish that can range in size from a foot to several feet long, has a mild flavor and addictive quality. And then there is its distinctive crunch. Fermented, it turns slightly soured and tangy but retains its snap. Serve this pickled daikon with an Asian-style meal to add healthy probiotics and a whole lot of flavor.

1 pound daikon
1 thumb-size piece of ginger
2 small dried Thai chiles or similar spicy chiles
1½ tablespoons pickling salt
2 cups water

1. Prepare the daikon by washing it under cool water to remove any dirt. Cut it into rounds about ¼-inch thick. Peel the ginger and cut it into several thin strips.

2. Layer the daikon in the jar, along with the ginger and chiles.

3. Dissolve the salt in the water, and pour over the daikon until it is covered.

4. Close the jar with either a lid or a lid with an air lock. If using a standard lid, be sure to open the jar slightly by unscrewing it every day to allow gas to escape before resealing it. Keep the jar at room temperature.

5. Begin tasting the daikon after 2 days, and leave it to ferment until it is as sour as you prefer. Once complete, cap the jar tightly and place in cold storage.

FERMENTED ZUCCHINI

MAKES: 1 QUART **PREP TIME:** 15 MINUTES **FERMENTATION TIME:** 1 TO 2 WEEKS

BEGINNER

At the height of summer, when your garden is at its peak, there are few things more plentiful than zucchini. Give this heavy producer new life as a ferment, and enjoy it for months to come. Use small zucchinis that still have tender skin to avoid peeling—this will save you prep time and retain more of the squash's nutrition. Grating the zucchini allows for a quick fermentation, but you can try other preparations as you desire. Try adding fermented zucchini to a fresh mixture of tomatoes and onions for a sour and salty tweak of a classic summer salad.

2 pounds zucchini
2 teaspoons pickling salt
2 cups water

1. Wash the zucchini under cool water. Grate the zucchini and pack it into a quart jar.

2. Dissolve the salt in the water. Pour the brine over the zucchini, filling the jar to about 2 inches from the top. Use a weight to hold the zucchini below the brine.

3. Cap the jar with an air lock if using. Otherwise, use a standard cap, being sure to open it every few days to allow built-up gas to escape.

4. Store in a cool location, and begin testing the fermented food after a week. When it becomes soured to your liking, cap the jar tightly and store the fermented zucchini in the refrigerator.

PICKLED GRAPE LEAVES

MAKES: 1 QUART **PREP TIME:** 15 MINUTES **FERMENTATION TIME:** 3 DAYS

BEGINNER

Pickled grape leaves are the cornerstone of the Mediterranean delight called dolmas (stuffed vegetable dishes). Traditionally stuffed with lamb, rice, and a blend of spices, these finger foods are always a treat. If you have a grapevine in your yard or have access to one, pluck several dozen leaves in midsummer while they are still tender yet have reached a formidable size. Removing a small amount of leaves does not hurt the vine or grapes but rather helps them. When they are removed around a cluster of grapes, it opens the canopy and allows the sun to better penetrate to the fruit for even ripening of the clusters.

36 grape leaves
2 tablespoons pickling salt
2 cups water

1. Wash the grape leaves using cool water. Dissolve the salt in the water in a bowl, and add the grape leaves to the bowl. Leave to soak for about 1 hour.

2. Working in groups of 6 leaves, roll the leaves together into a cylindrical shape, and place them vertically in the jar. Pack all the leaves into the jar in this way.

3. Pour the brine over the grape leaves. If the brine does not cover the grape leaves, make more using the same proportions of salt to water.

4. Cap the jar loosely and leave at room temperature for 3 days.

5. Cap the jar tightly. Transfer to cold storage for up to 2 weeks before using.

DILL PICKLES

MAKES: 2 QUARTS **PREP TIME:** 30 MINUTES **FERMENTATION TIME:** 4 WEEKS

INTERMEDIATE

One of the most basic pickles, the classic dill is always a crowd-pleaser. Salty and crisp, this pickle goes well on a sandwich or eaten on its own as a snack. Use pickling cucumbers when making these to create a crunchy pickle that stands up well to the fermentation process. Pickling cucumbers are typically available at markets and grocery stores during the peak season in midsummer, and this easy fermentation method allows you to keep tasty homemade pickles on hand year-round.

2½ pounds pickling cucumbers
  (3 to 5 inches each)

3 to 5 grape leaves

3 dill heads and a small handful of dill fronds

8 garlic cloves, peeled

1 dried chile, slit lengthwise

½ teaspoon peppercorns

3½ tablespoons pickling salt

5 cups water

1. Clean the cucumbers by gently rinsing them under running water. Remove the blossom ends of the cucumbers.

2. Place the grape leaves at the bottom of a jar. Layer the cucumbers in the jar along with the dill, garlic, and spices.

3. Dissolve the salt in the water, and pour the brine over the cucumbers. Use a weight, such as a clean rock, glass jar insert, or votive candleholder, to keep the cucumbers submerged in the brine.

4. Cover the jar with a clean kitchen towel, and store it in your kitchen at room temperature.

5. Bubbles should begin forming within a few days. Check daily for scum on the surface of the pickles, and if present, skim it off using a nonreactive utensil.

6. When the bubbles stop rising, after about 4 weeks, the pickles are ready. Pour the pickles from the jar into a colander placed over a pot. Remove the leaves, dill, garlic, and spices.

7. Bring the brine to a boil, and simmer it for 5 minutes. Skim off any scum that forms.

Continued

DILL PICKLES

CONTINUED

8. Rinse the pickles under cold water, and allow them to drain.

9. Cool the brine to room temperature, and pack the pickles back into a clean half-gallon jar or two quart jars. Pour the cooled brine over the pickles to cover them. Cap the jar with a nonreactive lid, and refrigerate the pickles for up to 6 months.

A CLOSER LOOK

Leaves of various plants are traditionally used in fermented pickle recipes to maintain a firm texture and ensure a bright green pickle. This result is produced by the tannins in the leaves of the plants. The recipes in this book all call for grape leaves when a firming agent is used. But sour cherry or oak leaves can be used to achieve the same effect.

FERMENTED PICKLE TROUBLESHOOTING

PROBLEM	POTENTIAL CAUSE
Shriveled pickles Soft pickles Pickles with brown spots	Although not as appetizing as they might be, these pickles are still edible. The issues all typically occur when the cucumbers are held too long before processing. Processing cucumbers within 2 days of picking them should prevent these issues from occurring.
Dark pickles	Although not beautiful, these pickles are still edible. Darkening can occur when pickling water contains a lot of iron or is alkaline. It can also occur due to contact with reactive metals during production.
Mushy, slippery pickles	Don't eat these! Mushy pickles indicate that food-spoiling microbes have grown on your pickles. This can occur because too little salt was used, the pickles weren't fully submerged during fermentation, the blossom ends of the cucumbers weren't removed, or the brine was not skimmed. Toss the batch.
Off-flavors	This is also an indication that undesirable microbes grew in the pickles due to the same reasons listed in the preceding entry. But as long as the pickles are sour, not mushy (soft is okay), and free of mold, they are safe for consumption.
Hollow middles	Although not as appetizing as they might be, these pickles are still edible. Inadequate watering often produces cucumbers with hollow middles, as does holding cucumbers too long before processing. Before processing, you can find and discard the cucumbers with hollow middles by submerging them in water: They will float to the surface.

HALF SOURS

INTERMEDIATE

Half sours pack all the punch of a pickle but still retain some of their original attributes. With a little more crunch than the typical dill, half sours walk the line between pickle and raw cucumber. Cured quickly in a lower-salt brine, these pickles never get as sour as other types of fermented pickles, and are a perfect place to start for those who don't normally like the puckering sour flavor of pickled foods.

¼ pound pickling cucumbers
1 garlic clove, crushed
1 dill head
1 chile, slit lengthwise
¼ teaspoon peppercorns, coarsely crushed
1½ tablespoons pickling salt
3 cups water

1. Clean the cucumbers under cold running water to remove any dirt on their surface. Remove the blossom end of each cucumber.

2. Pack the garlic, dill head, and spices into the jar, layering them with the cucumbers.

3. Dissolve the salt in the water, and pour the brine over the cucumbers.

4. Place a small weight into the jar to hold the cucumbers below the surface of the brine, and cover the jar with a clean kitchen towel. Store the jar at room temperature.

5. Bubbles should begin to form within 3 days, signifying the start of fermentation. When this occurs, check daily for scum on the surface of the brine. If any appears, skim it off immediately with a nonreactive utensil.

6. Half sours are typically done in about a week—when they develop a distinctively sour flavor and bubbles stop rising to the top. Skim off any scum in the jar, affix a nonreactive top, and store the pickles in the refrigerator for at least 3 days before eating. These pickles should be eaten within 3 weeks of being moved to the refrigerator.

MUSTARD AND HORSERADISH DILLS

MAKES: 2 QUARTS **PREP TIME:** 15 MINUTES **FERMENTATION TIME:** 2 TO 3 WEEKS

INTERMEDIATE

If you like a dill pickle with a little kick, this is your recipe. Pairing the complementary piquant flavors of mustard and horseradish, this is a lovely fermenting project that takes a big flavor leap beyond the ordinary. Because these last for up to 4 months when refrigerated, make a half gallon at once and enjoy these special pickles at your leisure.

2 pounds pickling cucumbers

4 to 5 grape leaves

½ cup raw horseradish, chopped

2 tablespoons mustard seeds

2 heads fresh dill

3 tablespoons pickling salt

4 cups water

1. Wash the cucumbers under cold running water to remove any debris. Remove the blossom ends.

2. Place the grape leaves at the bottom of the jar. Layer the cucumbers, horseradish, mustard seeds, and dill into the jar.

3. Mix the salt and water until the salt is dissolved. Pour the brine over the cucumbers until covered.

4. Use a weight to submerge the pickles, and cover the jar with a clean kitchen towel. Store at room temperature.

5. Fermentation should be visible within 3 days, when tiny bubbles form on the surface. If scum appears, skim it off daily with a nonreactive utensil. Rinse the scum off the weights when present.

6. When bubbling stops—in about 2 to 3 weeks—the pickles are done. Remove the weight, close the jar with a nonreactive lid, and refrigerate for up to 4 months.

FENNEL PICKLES

MAKES: 2 QUARTS **PREP TIME:** 15 MINUTES **FERMENTATION TIME:** 2 TO 3 WEEKS

INTERMEDIATE

If you are not a fan of dill, don't count out cucumber pickles just yet. There are many ways to pickle that omit this seemingly ubiquitous seasoning. Using a mixture of black pepper, lemon, and fennel, this pickle has sour notes similar to those of the traditional dill, but with a new and inviting twist. Once you master this recipe, do not hesitate to throw in some of your preferred spices to create a unique-to-you favorite with your most prized seasonings.

2 pounds small pickling cucumbers

3 to 5 grape leaves

2 teaspoons peppercorns

Zest of 1 lemon, cut into strips

2 fresh fennel heads (if available) or
   1 tablespoon fennel seeds

2 tablespoons white vinegar

3 tablespoons pickling salt

1 quart water

1. Clean the cucumbers under cool water to remove any dirt. Remove the blossom end of each cucumber.

2. Place the grape leaves in the bottom of the jar. Pack the cucumbers into the jar, layering them with the peppercorns, lemon zest, and fennel.

3. Dissolve the vinegar and salt in the water, and pour the brine over the cucumbers until they are covered. Use a weight to hold the vegetables below the surface. Place a standard cap, a cap with an air lock, or a freezer bag filled with the remaining brine in the jar to seal it. Store the jar at room temperature.

4. After 3 days, fermentation should be noticeable as tiny bubbles rising in the jar. Begin to check the pickles daily for scum on the surface. Should any appear, skim it off with a nonreactive utensil and replace the cap. If using a standard cap, be sure to unscrew the lid every day or every other day to allow gases to escape.

5. When the bubbles stop rising, fermentation is complete. This can take anywhere from 2 to 3 weeks, at which point, the pickles will be sour throughout.

Continued

FENNEL PICKLES

CONTINUED

6. Remove the pickles from the jar by pouring them into a colander placed over a pot to collect the brine.

7. Bring the brine to a boil, and simmer for 5 minutes. If scum forms, skim it off. Let it cool to room temperature.

8. While the brine is coming to a boil, remove the peppercorns, lemon zest, and fennel from the pickles, and rinse the pickles well under cold water.

9. Pack the pickles back into a 2-quart jar, and once cooled, pour the brine to cover the pickles. Place in cold storage for up to 6 months.

QUICK-FERMENTED CHINESE CABBAGE

MAKES: 2 QUARTS **PREP TIME:** 15 MINUTES, 1 DAY DRYING (OPTIONAL)
FERMENTATION TIME: 2 TO 4 DAYS

INTERMEDIATE

This simple fermented Chinese cabbage is a lovely accompaniment to both Asian-style meals and Western ones. Traditionally made in a large wooden tub, this delicate pickle, flavored with just lemon and kombu, is consumed all winter long in Japan, where it originates. Select a Chinese cabbage that is heavy for its size and has no black spots on its leaves.

1 small head Chinese cabbage (about 5 pounds)
1 lemon
1 (8-inch) piece of kombu seaweed
3½ tablespoons salt

1. Remove and reserve the outer leaves of the cabbage. Split the cabbage in half vertically, and then split each half in half again vertically to create 4 quarters. Trim off the tough portion of the base.

2. Weather permitting, sun-dry the cabbage for 1 day to bring out its natural sweetness. If the weather does not allow this, skip this step and proceed with the recipe.

3. Cut the lemon into thin rounds. Cut the kombu into several strips.

4. Measure the salt and sprinkle ½ tablespoon into the bottom of a large nonreactive bowl. Pack 1 or 2 of the cabbage wedges in the bowl, and sprinkle with some of the remaining salt. Layer the remaining ingredients in a similar fashion, placing a few rounds of lemon, more strips of kombu, another cabbage wedge, and another sprinkling of salt, repeating the layering of salt, kombu, and lemon until all the prepared ingredients have been used.

Continued

5. Cover the cabbage with the reserved outer leaves. Place a plate that fits in the bowl onto the surface of the cabbage to function as a Japanese-style "drop-lid." Apply a weight that is approximately double the weight of the cabbage on top of the plate (a couple of quart jars filled with water and then capped would work well). Cover with a clean kitchen towel, and store in a cool location.

6. After 1 day, remove the weight and turn over the cabbage pieces. Let the cabbage stand, weighted down, for 1 to 3 more days before eating.

A CLOSER LOOK

Because this is a quick-pickled type of fermented food, it is not protected by brine, unlike other methods of fermentation. For this reason, it is more prone to growing mold on its surface if left for an extended period or placed in a hot location. To avoid spoilage, be sure to store this ferment in a cool area, and once finished, put it in an airtight container and refrigerate for up to 3 days.

BRAN-FERMENTED VEGETABLES

THE BRAN PICKLING BED PRODUCES LIGHTLY FERMENTED PICKLES EVERY 12 TO 72 HOURS

PREP TIME: 30 MINUTES **FERMENTATION TIME:** 12 TO 72 HOURS

ADVANCED

At one time, every Japanese household had a crock of these vegetables stored somewhere in its kitchen, typically beneath the floor, where the temperature stayed cool year-round. The rice bran pickling mixture was unique to each household; it was traditionally passed down from generation to generation. Because the pickling bed must be tended daily, making these pickles at home has fallen out of favor in recent generations. Pickles created by burying vegetables in the pickling bed are called *nukamiso-zuke*, and they end up being just as unique as the home where they were created. Because rice bran can be difficult to source, this recipe allows for oat or wheat bran, each of which produce slightly different but similarly delicious results. You will need a large container or 1-gallon pickling crock to make this recipe.

½ cup pickling salt

4 cups water

1 slice white bread

1 (4-inch) piece of dried kombu seaweed

2 pounds rice, oat, or wheat bran

¼ cup mustard powder

¼ cup dried soybeans

1 (1-inch) piece ginger, sliced

2 red chiles

Vegetable scraps, for testing

Vegetables for pickling, such as small whole cucumbers, eggplant, turnips, carrots, cabbage, daikon, and cauliflower

1. Add the salt and water to a small pan, and heat until the salt is dissolved. Remove from heat and cool to room temperature.

2. Tear the bread into small pieces, and add to the water-salt mixture.

3. Use a wet cloth to wipe the surface of the kombu. Use kitchen scissors to cut the kombu in half.

4. Add ⅓ of the bran to the pickling container, and mix together with the mustard powder and ½ of the soybeans.

Continued

5. Mix in about ¼ of the brine and bread pieces, and stir until smooth and the blend has the texture of wet sand. Add more of the bran and the remaining soybeans, ginger slices, and chiles. Mix well.

6. Continue to add the bran and brine-and-bread mixture, ¼ of each at a time, to the pickling container until the consistency is moist but not runny—add only as much brine as needed to maintain the wet, sandlike texture. Add the kombu.

7. Bury a couple of vegetable scraps in the mixture for testing. Pat the surface of the bran flat once the vegetables are buried, and use a wet cloth to remove any bran along the inner edges of the container. Cover the container with a clean kitchen towel.

8. After 12 hours, try the scraps. If they still have a raw taste, bury them again for a longer period of time, for up to 2 days. Once they have become pickled to your liking, remove the scraps. Snack on them or discard.

9. To bury new vegetables in the pickling bed, first wash them under cool water and pat them dry. For hard vegetables, such as daikon or carrots, slice them to accelerate pickling time. Rub the vegetables lightly with salt, and bury them in the pickling bed. Always press down the surface of the pickling bed, wipe the inner edges of the container with a wet cloth, and cover the container with a clean kitchen towel. Leave vegetables for at least 12 hours and up to 3 days, based on the types of vegetables and your own taste preferences.

BRAN-FERMENTED PICKLING TIPS

- It is best to prepare a bran pickling bed in early spring to early summer, so you are able to allow plenty of time for it to mature before fresh produce is available for pickling. It generally takes 3 to 4 weeks for the bran pickling bed to mature and be able to yield the best-tasting pickled vegetables. During this time, stir it daily, even if no vegetables are added to the mixture.

- Be sure that you always remove all remnants of vegetables once pickled. Even tiny amounts can release liquid and cause the bed to become sour.

- If the pickling bed becomes too sour, add a little mustard powder to the bran to help neutralize the acid.

- If the bran becomes too watery due to liquid released by the vegetables, add a bit more bran mixed with salt and mustard powder to it, stirring until the new bran mixture is thoroughly incorporated.

- Always check the entire bed once a week to remove any leftover vegetables that may have been missed. If you find yourself with overly salty vegetables, soak them in water to remove excess salt.

- If mold grows on the surface of the pickling bed, which typically occurs only when the pickling bed is not stirred for too long a period, scrape off the affected bran, wipe the inner edges of the container with a wet cloth, and replace the kitchen towel.

- To store the pickling bed during long periods of dormancy, transfer the bran to a plastic bag that is loosely tied, so that it will allow some air to get inside. Place in the refrigerator. When ready to reuse, bring the mixture to room temperature, add bran, salt, and kombu to adjust the consistency, and test vegetables again until you get good results.

4

FRUITS

Fruit has a relatively short shelf life. Leave it sitting too long on the counter, and you are in for a rotten mess, not to mention the most annoying and dreaded of kitchen pests, fruit flies. Refrigerate it and the texture often changes, leaving you with an equally undesirable product.

This is where fermentation shines. In return for a little work, you are able to produce a concoction that has a longer shelf life, as well as different flavors and complexities. Although you may not want to eat all those apples off your tree in autumn, they sure will taste great in spring, when fresh apples will not be available for several more months. The same goes for berries, peaches, plums, and all of summer's other amazing treats.

Whey or other starters are most commonly used for fruit ferments, as they do not impart a flavor as strong and salty as a brine, which is typically incompatible with the sweet notes of fruit.

Fruit ferments are trickier to manage than vegetable ferments. The sugar in fruit can easily turn into alcohol if the fermented food is left unattended for too long or if the fruit is fermented at too high a temperature. The upside is that fruit ferments are generally quick to process, taking no more than a few days from start to completion, and they require no special equipment.

All of the recipes in this chapter can be made using either pint or quart mason jars. If you have pickling jars with air locks, these can be used, although they are not necessary.

When available, choose fresh organic fruits for pickling. In a pinch, frozen fruits can be used for cooked recipes, such as jam, but be sure to read the labels to ensure that no additional ingredients have been added.

STARTER CULTURES

Ideally, you will use homemade yogurt or milk kefir to obtain the whey for these ferments. But if these are not available, you can also use store-bought, plain, whole milk yogurt to get your whey. Follow the same process outlined on page (23) to obtain whey from your favorite store-bought, plain, whole milk yogurt.

If you are lactose-intolerant, whey may not be the best option for you, as it does contain a small amount of lactose. Instead, you can substitute an equal amount of brine from a previous ferment, such as sauerkraut, or use an equal amount of kombucha or plain water kefir. Keep in mind that fermented vegetable brines, such as those from sauerkraut, have a distinct taste of their own and may not be suitable for all fruit ferments.

BLACKBERRY-SAGE JAM

MAKES: 1 QUART **PREP TIME:** 15 MINUTES **FERMENTATION TIME:** 2 DAYS

BEGINNER

The sweetness of blackberries is complemented by a subtle note of sage in this stunning jam. Lacto-fermentation using whey adds character to the jam, which is made in the same way your grandmother may have made it. Honey sweetens the jam and the fruit's natural pectin helps firm it up for the desired consistency. Once you make this a couple of times, experiment with different berries for unique ingredient combinations.

5 cups blackberries, divided
1 cup honey
2 teaspoons sea salt
¼ cup fresh sage leaves, roughly chopped
2 teaspoons lemon juice
¼ cup whey (page 23)

1. Stir together 3 cups of the blackberries, honey, and salt in a medium nonreactive saucepan over low heat until the berries begin to release their juices. Using the back of a spoon or a potato masher, crush the blackberries as they soften and mix well with the honey. Set aside to cool.

2. In a blender, purée the remaining 2 cups of blackberries, the sage leaves, and the lemon juice.

3. Once the cooked berries have cooled, pour them, the puréed berries, and the whey into a clean pint jar.

4. Cover the jar and leave it at room temperature for 2 days. Then transfer to the refrigerator, where it will keep for 1 month.

PAIR IT

Blackberry-sage jam is a versatile condiment with many uses at the table. Mix it with homemade Yogurt (page 87) and Granola (page 180) for a fruity breakfast, or use it to top waffles, Kefir Biscuits (page 178), or Oatmeal Pancakes (page 179) in place of syrup. Or make a glaze using jam, white wine vinegar, and crushed garlic to spread on a roast for a sweet-and-savory take on a traditional dinner.

APPLE BUTTER

MAKES: 1 QUART   **PREP TIME**: 30 MINUTES   **FERMENTATION TIME**: 2 DAYS

BEGINNER

Apple butter is a delicious treat when slathered on a piece of toast. This recipe not only tastes great but has a healthy probiotic tweak. Using dried apples, this treat is easy to make any time of the year, even when fresh, delicious apples are not in season. Look for unsulfured dried apples to ensure that fermentation is not slowed—added sulphur, a preservative, interferes with the fermentation process.

2 cups dried apples
Water
1½ teaspoons sea salt
2 tablespoons whey (page 23)
2 tablespoons honey

1. Add the dried apples to a medium saucepan. Fill the pan with water, and simmer the apples in the water until they reconstitute. Allow the apples to cool slightly.

2. Transfer the apples to a food processor using a slotted spoon, and add the remaining ingredients. Process until smooth.

3. Pour into a quart jar and cap tightly. Allow it to stand at room temperature for 2 days. Transfer to cold storage, where it can be kept for up to 2 months.

CRANBERRY CHUTNEY

MAKES: 1 QUART **PREP TIME:** 10 MINUTES **FERMENTATION TIME:** 2 DAYS

BEGINNER

Cranberries are a nutritional power-house, rich in vitamin C, fiber, and manganese. Why settle for the canned version of this holiday treat? You can make your own at home and take advantage of its good-for-you probiotic content at the same time. And this is perhaps the best part—no one will ever know you swapped the usual stuff for this healthier recipe. The fermented nature of this chutney is almost unnoticeable, making it the perfect way to incorporate some healthy bacteria into the diets of those who are squeamish about fermented foods.

4 cups fresh cranberries

1 medium orange, seeded and chopped

⅔ cup honey

½ cup whey (page 23)

1 teaspoon ground cinnamon

1 teaspoon minced fresh ginger

1. Rinse the cranberries and pick out any that are discolored or spoiled.

2. Add all the ingredients to a blender or food processor, and lightly process until still chunky.

3. Transfer to a quart jar and cap tightly.

4. Leave on the counter at room temperature for 2 days.

5. Transfer to the refrigerator, where it will keep for 2 months.

A CLOSER LOOK

Cranberries are typically available fresh only around Thanksgiving and Christmas. But if you enjoy this ferment, there is no reason not to make it year-round. Stock up on cranberries when they are in season, and freeze them in their original packaging to have them on hand when you want them. When you are ready to make this chutney, thaw the cranberries and proceed as usual.

PEACH CHUTNEY

MAKES: 1 PINT **PREP TIME:** 15 MINUTES **FERMENTATION TIME:** 2 DAYS

BEGINNER

Chutney is a versatile condiment that typically contains sweet and spicy elements. Serve this seasonal peach chutney along with meat, such as chicken or pork, for a flavorful new take on a favorite dish, or eat it with tender grilled fish for the perfect balance of smoky, salty, spicy, and sweet.

Juice of 1 lemon

Grated rind of 1 lemon

1 teaspoon sea salt

2 tablespoons whey (page 23)

¼ cup water

1½ cups peeled and diced fresh peaches
  (about 2 medium peaches)

¼ cup raisins

¼ cup pecans

½ teaspoon ground cumin

½ teaspoon fennel seeds

½ teaspoon ground coriander

¼ teaspoon white peppercorns

1½ teaspoons honey

1. Add the lemon juice, lemon rind, salt, whey, and water to a pint jar. Add the diced peaches to the mixture and stir well.

2. Add the raisins, pecans, spices, and honey to the jar, pressing down slightly with a spoon to ensure the fruit mixture is below the rim of the jar.

3. If the liquid has not risen to the top of the jar, add a bit more water. Cap the jar tightly and leave it out at room temperature for 2 days.

4. Transfer to the refrigerator, where it will keep for 2 months.

WATERMELON SALSA

MAKES: 1 QUART **PREP TIME:** 15 MINUTES **FERMENTATION TIME:** 12 HOURS

BEGINNER

This juicy, fruity condiment is a sweet and refreshing treat on a summer day. It can be paired with tortilla chips for a novel approach to the traditional appetizer, or added to fish tacos as a delightful complement. For the adventurous, it makes a delicious cold soup on a hot day.

3 cups diced watermelon

⅓ cup fresh cilantro, chopped finely

1 cup chopped red onion

1½ teaspoons sea salt

⅛ cup each fresh mint and basil, mixed together and chopped finely

⅛ teaspoon ground cumin

¼ teaspoon red pepper flakes

1. Add all the ingredients to a nonreactive bowl and mix thoroughly. Pack into a quart jar and press down with a spoon to extract enough juice to cover the fruit. Use a weight to hold the watermelon below the liquid.

2. Cap the jar with a standard lid or a lid fitted with an air lock, and leave at room temperature.

3. Ferment for up to 12 hours, and then transfer to cold storage.

LACTO-FERMENTED BERRIES

MAKES: 1 PINT PREP TIME: 5 MINUTES FERMENTATION TIME: 12 TO 24 HOURS

BEGINNER

Fermented berries are a perfect topping for desserts, cereals, and granola, adding amazing flavor as well as probiotic benefits. This recipe can be used for all types of berries, with the exception of strawberries, which do not ferment well due to their high acid content. Try this simple recipe with boysenberries, blackberries, raspberries, blueberries, or any mixture of these berries.

2 cups fresh berries
2 tablespoons honey
¼ teaspoon sea salt
2 tablespoons whey (page 23)
Water

1. Place the berries in a pint jar, and gently press them down with your clean fist or a spoon.

2. Mix the honey, sea salt, and whey in a measuring cup, and pour the mixture over the berries.

3. Gently press the fruit down into the liquid and add water as needed to cover it, as the fruit must be submerged in the liquid to properly ferment. Use a weight to hold the berries below the surface (as described on page 22), and add a cap to the jar.

4. Ferment at room temperature for 12 to 24 hours, until the fruit is slightly soured and has a hint of carbonation.

5. Transfer to the refrigerator, where it can be stored for up to 2 months.

CINNAMON SPICED APPLES

MAKES: 1 QUART **PREP TIME**: 10 MINUTES, 45 MINUTES COOLING **FERMENTATION TIME**: 7 DAYS

BEGINNER

Bring home the taste of fall with this delicious apple preparation, which retains some of the fruit's naturally crisp texture. Spiced with hints of cinnamon, this nostalgic flavor combination works as well for a simple midday snack as it does for a topping on a seasonal salad. Use your favorite variety of apple, or mix and match several types for more nuanced complexity.

1 organic lemon
2 cinnamon sticks
2 tablespoons salt
3 cups water
2 medium apples

1. Wash and slice the lemon, and break the cinnamon stick into several pieces.

2. Combine the salt, water, lemon slices, and cinnamon stick pieces in a small saucepan. Heat over medium-high and bring to a simmer in order to infuse the liquid with cinnamon flavor and dissolve the salt. Cool to room temperature.

3. Wash and dry the apples, and then halve and core them. Slice the apples thinly, leaving the skin on.

4. Pack the apple slices into a quart jar, and top with the cooled brine. Use a weight to hold the apples below the brine. Cover loosely with a lid, and leave at room temperature for up to 7 days, or until fermentation stops.

5. Close the lid tightly and transfer the jar to cold storage, where the contents will keep for several months.

LACTO-FERMENTED RASPBERRY SAUCE

MAKES: 1 PINT PREP TIME: 15 MINUTES FERMENTATION TIME: 1 TO 3 DAYS

BEGINNER

Drizzle this sweet, vibrant red sauce over ice cream, pancakes, or yogurt, and take your meal from ordinary to extraordinary. This is simple to make, and its probiotics transform an otherwise decadent pleasure into a healthy, gut-loving masterpiece. Although fresh is always best, frozen berries work great in this recipe, where texture is not an issue. If you are not a fan of raspberries, try the same recipe with similar fruits, such as blackberries, boysenberries, or blueberries.

2 cups raspberries
3 tablespoons raw honey
4 tablespoons whey, divided (page 23)

1. Using a potato masher, mash the raspberries well. Mix in the honey and 2 tablespoons of the whey.

2. Transfer the mixture to a pint jar. Pour the remaining 2 tablespoons of whey over the surface of the sauce and seal the jar. Keep the jar at room temperature for 1 to 3 days.

3. Check the jar daily and loosen the top to release built-up gas. When bubbles are visible in the jar, cap it tightly and transfer to cold storage. The contents are best when used within 5 days.

KUMQUAT MARMALADE

BEGINNER

Kumquats, which already contain both sour and sweet flavors, are taken to another level in fermented marmalade. Whether on toast, biscuits, or English muffins, this simple spread has a unique, eye-opening flavor. Unlike other citrus fruits, kumquats are eaten with the skin on, giving this marmalade a desirable texture that, because it is raw, is slightly runnier than the standard cooked version.

2 cups thinly sliced kumquats
1½ teaspoons salt
2 tablespoons whey (page 23)
¼ cup water
¼ cup sugar

1. If seeds are present in the kumquats, remove them carefully before proceeding to the next step.

2. Pack the kumquats into a pint jar.

3. Mix the remaining ingredients until the salt and sugar are dissolved, and pour over the sliced fruit. Press the kumquats down into the jar to release their juices. If the kumquats are not covered in liquid, add as much water as necessary until they are completely submerged. Close the jar with a standard lid, and leave out at room temperature.

4. After 3 days, transfer the jar to cold storage.

A CLOSER LOOK

Kumquats, which look like grape-size citrus, are high in vitamin C as well as antioxidants, polyphenols, and beta-carotene. These compounds support a healthy immune system. Prepare this marmalade in the winter, when fresh fruit choices are lackluster, and enjoy its immune-boosting benefits.

PRESERVED LEMON

MAKES: 1 QUART **PREP TIME:** 15 MINUTES **FERMENTATION TIME:** 2 TO 4 WEEKS

BEGINNER

Many cultures use lemon pickles to add a distinctive flavor to their cuisine. This simple pickle can be added to a Moroccan tagine, served alongside a traditional Indian meal, or substituted for lemon zest in a variety of dishes. Because the entire lemon, including its rind, is fermented, it is important to select organic lemons for this project.

7 or 8 organic lemons
1 cup salt

1. Soak the lemons in lightly soapy water and scrub clean. Rinse thoroughly and dry.

2. Trim the stem end of the lemons. Cut 5 of the lemons into quarters, and pack them into a clean quart jar. Pour the salt around the lemons as you add them to the jar, fully coating each piece. They should fit tightly in the jar. If not, add additional lemon quarters until the citrus is tightly packed into the jar.

3. Cut an additional 2 lemons in half, and squeeze all of their juice over the top of the fruit already in the container. Press the lemons down so that they are covered with juice. Use another lemon if necessary. Add any remaining salt.

4. Cover the jar using a plastic lid. Don't use a metal canning lid, as the salt would corrode the surface of the lid.

5. Leave the lemons at room temperature for at least 2 weeks before transferring them to cold storage.

TRY INSTEAD

If you don't have a plastic lid, then cover the canning jar with a piece of plastic wrap to prevent the salt and acid in the lemon from rusting or eating away at the lid. In a pinch, this simple fix can be used with any acidic pickle or ferment to prevent corrosion.

STRAWBERRY CHIA JAM

MAKES 1 PINT **PREP TIME:** 10 MINUTES **FERMENTATION TIME:** 2 DAYS

BEGINNER

Yes, these are the same chia seeds that you may remember from the grass-growing clay pet of your youth. Consumed as far back as Mayan and Atzec civilations, chia seeds are a natural energy booster loaded with antioxidants, fiber, and calcium. These tiny seeds, which become gelatinous in liquid, help to firm up this simple raw jam, as well as give you a boost of heart-healthy omega-3s.

2½ cups strawberries
½ cup honey
1 teaspoon sea salt
3 tablespoons chia seeds
2 tablespoons whey (page 23)

1. Place all the ingredients in a blender jar and process until they are your desired consistency.

2. Pour the jam into a pint jar and cover the jar with a lid. Leave at room temperature for 2 days. Transfer the jam to the refrigerator where it will keep for one month.

PREPARATION TIP

Chia seeds give a different look to jam, as even when using a blender, the seeds remain somewhat intact. If you don't like the idea of "spotty" jam, grind the chia seeds on their own using a mortar and pestle or clean coffee grinder before adding them to the blender.

5

DAIRY

In the Western world, going to the grocery store, purchasing milk, and then bringing it home to store in an electric refrigerator is a routine activity. Milk is seamlessly transported from farm to grocery store, and most consumers give little thought to the distance the milk travels. Even today, this is not the case for many people around the world, who live without electricity or refrigeration.

Dairy fermentation developed out of the need to extend the life of milk, a commodity that is no longer fresh after sitting for just a few hours at room temperature.

In some cultures, fermented products continue to be the leading way that dairy is regularly consumed, thousands of years after these products were originally created. Yogurt originated in the Middle East more than 4,500 years ago, kefir is purported to have existed in Central Asia since 3000 BC, and cheese predates them all, with origins stretching to 5500 BC in Poland.

If the idea of fermenting dairy seems scary, have no fear. Modern culture has dictated that milk must be refrigerated at all times to keep it safe, but in reality, fermenting these products is a completely safe practice when done properly. People have been fermenting dairy for centuries, and there is little need to be concerned with foodborne illness when you follow the step-by-step directions laid out here.

Many dairy ferments can be made at home with little specialized equipment, and those ferments are the focus of this chapter. Although there are many outstanding cheeses that you can make in your own kitchen, many of them require special supplies, which add to the cost of your project considerably. This chapter includes a variety of simple dairy ferments that can be made with basic items found in a well-stocked kitchen.

A WORD ON MILK

Dairy ferments begin with milk or sometimes cream, and choosing the right products can help determine the success of your handiwork. Although the ferments in this chapter all use full-fat dairy, don't let that discourage you from trying them if you are on a low-fat diet. Low-fat milk products can be substituted in these recipes, but they will yield slightly different results in the consistency of the finished product.

One crucial thing is to select pasteurized milk and not ultra-high-temperature pasteurized milk, also known as UHT milk. Because UHT milk is processed at 275°F or higher, compared to 161°F for traditionally pasteurized milk, it is not a viable choice for cultured milk products. Raw milk may also be used instead of pasteurized milk. But because raw milk has plenty of beneficial bacteria of its own, these bacteria may compete with the culturing medium and the process may take longer.

Cow's milk is the most widely available type of milk, but it is not your only option. Goat's milk can be substituted, but due to a slightly different structure, it typically produces cultured products that are thinner than cow's milk–based items. Sheep's milk, on the other hand, is sweeter and contains more protein than cow's milk, resulting in a thicker and creamier texture. If you are lucky enough to have a local source for sheep's milk, give it a try.

KEFIR

Forget about expensive grocery store bottles of kefir, and make this simple drink yourself with practically no effort. Kefir is a well-loved, creamy dairy ferment, and is loaded with many more strains of beneficial bacteria than a standard yogurt. Slightly soured, and comparable to a drinkable yogurt or buttermilk, kefir can be made using cow's, goat's, or sheep's milk. Each will yield slightly different results in terms of thickness and creaminess, but each will be delicious in its own right. Whole milk provides the best consistency in the finished product. Low-fat milk also works well but creates a thinner kefir. Try kefir plain, use it in cooking (try our Kefir Biscuits, page 178), or flavor it with other ingredients to enjoy this glorious traditional beverage. Using just milk and kefir "grains" (not true grains, so no need to avoid this fermented food if you are on a gluten-free diet), this is a project that requires minimal effort but comes out great every time.

1 to 2 tablespoons kefir grains
1 quart milk

1. Add the kefir grains to a 1-quart jar. Fill the remainder of the jar with the milk (see fig. A).

2. Cover the jar using a clean cloth secured with a rubber band (see fig. B). Allow it to sit at room temperature for 12 to 24 hours. For the most flavor, thickness, and bacteria, culture for the full 24 hours, at which time the kefir will have developed a much denser texture. If you prefer a thinner kefir, end fermentation at 12 hours.

3. Strain out the grains using a nonreactive (preferably plastic) strainer placed over another quart jar to capture the kefir (see fig. C).

4. Place a lid on the jar, and store it in the refrigerator.

5. Reuse the kefir grains in another quart of milk to start the process over again.

Continued

5

DAIRY

GOING WITH THE GRAINS

Rehydrating Kefir Grains

When starting with dehydrated grains, they must first be rehydrated before preparing kefir. To do this, empty the contents of your dehydrated milk kefir grains into 1 cup of cold, pasteurized milk. Cover the cup with a coffee filter or clean towel, secured by a rubber band, and place it in a location that ranges from 68°F to 85°F. After 24 hours, if the milk is not thickened, strain out the kefir grains, and place them in a fresh cup of milk. Repeat this process until the milk thickens within 24 hours, which may take a few days. When it reaches this stage, increase the amount of milk to 1½ cups and repeat the process. Continue increasing the amount of milk you add every day by ½ cup until you reach 4 cups of milk, at which point, the grains are hydrated and ready for use.

Kefir Grains vs. Powdered Kefir Starter Culture

If the prospect of making kefir daily sounds daunting, powdered kefir starter culture may be a better choice than grains to get you started. Powdered starter culture is designed for people who do not plan to make kefir regularly. The downside of this product is that it eventually loses efficacy and needs to be replaced. (The grains can continue to produce kefir indefinitely.) A small amount of kefir made using powdered starter culture can be saved to culture a subsequent batch of kefir within 7 days of being made. Powdered kefir starter culture costs only a fraction of the cost of kefir grains, but because they are indefinitely viable, kefir grains are in the long run more cost effective.

DAIRY

5

BERRY, BERRY FIZZY KEFIR

MAKES: 1 QUART **PREP TIME:** 10 MINUTES **FERMENTATION TIME:** 12 TO 24 HOURS

Using secondary fermentation (any additional fermentation time after the kefir grains are removed), you can infuse a whole host of flavors, such as fruit, spices, or other seasonings, into plain kefir to take this healthy beverage to another level. Secondary fermentation also decreases the lactose content in the final product, making it a beneficial practice for people with lactose sensitivity. During this stage, the air supply present during the initial fermentation is absent, creating a delightful effervescence in the finished drink.

½ cup raspberries
½ cup blackberries
½ cup blueberries
1 teaspoon vanilla extract
3 cups Kefir (page 79)

1. Purée the berries with the vanilla extract in a blender.

2. Add the berry mixture to the kefir. Put a lid on the jar, and let it sit in a warm location for an additional 12 to 24 hours. Open the jar to allow gas to escape, seal the lid tightly, and store the kefir in the refrigerator.

TRY INSTEAD

Kefir can be flavored using myriad spices and seasonings. Fruits produce a sweetened kefir, and ginger, cinnamon, and mint are complementary as well. Once you've got the basic recipe down, experiment with blends of your own. After all, the only thing that could go wrong is that you don't like it, in which case you can dump it and have a different batch ready in about 24 hours.

5

DAIRY

SAVORY DIGESTIVE KEFIR

MAKES: 1 QUART **PREP TIME:** 10 MINUTES **FERMENTATION TIME:** 12 TO 24 HOURS

BEGINNER

There is no need to stick solely with sweet tones. Equally as delicious with savory flavors, kefir can be transformed into a digestive tonic by adding a few key ingredients. Through secondary fermentation, this kefir will quickly become carbonated. This is a simple recipe that you can use as a baseline, so feel free to omit or add spices to create a drink that suits your tastes.

1 teaspoon fennel
1 teaspoon cumin seeds
1 quart Kefir (page 79)
1 (1-inch) knob of ginger

1. Using a spice grinder or coffee grinder, process the fennel and cumin into a powder. Add this to the kefir.

2. Peel and mince the ginger. Gather the pieces in a small piece of cheesecloth. Squeeze the ginger's juice into the kefir.

3. Place a lid on the jar, and leave it in a warm location for 12 to 24 hours. Open the jar to allow built-up gases to escape, seal it tightly, and place the finished drink in the refrigerator.

A CLOSER LOOK

The best way to keep kefir grains alive is to use them daily, but this is not always possible. To take a break from using your grains for up to 3 weeks, store them in a quart of milk in a tightly sealed jar in the refrigerator. The cold temperature will greatly slow fermentation. For a break of up to 6 months, rinse the grains and dry them at room temperature or in a dehydrator at less than 85°F. Place the grains in a freezer storage bag with a little powdered milk, and store them in the refrigerator for up to 6 months. Rehydrate before use.

SOUR KEFIR CREAM

MAKES: 1 PINT **PREP TIME:** 5 MINUTES **FERMENTATION TIME:** 12 TO 18 HOURS

BEGINNER

One of the best things about fermentation is that it is self-perpetuating. Once you get started making ferments, you have the tools to make more and more projects, such as this sour cream recipe, without a store-bought starter culture. Using just a small amount of homemade yogurt or kefir, you can quickly and inexpensively turn cream into a slightly sour, lusciously thickened condiment with no additional ingredients.

2 cups heavy cream
1 tablespoon yogurt or Kefir (page 79)

1. Mix the cream and yogurt or kefir together in a jar.

2. Cover the jar with a clean kitchen towel, and secure it with a rubber band.

3. Place it in a warm location, ranging from 70°F to 77°F. After 12 to 18 hours, check on the cream. Once it is thickened to your liking, put a lid on the jar.

4. For the best results, store the sour kefir cream in the refrigerator for at least 6 hours before using.

TRY INSTEAD

Although heavy cream will yield the thickest sour cream, for a lower fat version, try making this recipe with half-and-half instead. The end product will be slightly thinner, but this can be amended by adding a bit of dry milk powder to the mixture to thicken it to your desired consistency.

CULTURED BUTTERMILK

MAKES: 1 QUART **PREP TIME:** 15 MINUTES **FERMENTATION TIME:** 12 TO 24 HOURS

BEGINNER

DAIRY

A favorite for baking, buttermilk has a distinctive tang all its own. Another simple product easily created in your kitchen, this recipe can be made using a store-bought starter culture or by purchasing cultured buttermilk from the store and using a bit of it to get a new batch going. Whichever method you prefer, this simple method will give you a product that adds just the right flavor to buttermilk pancakes or biscuits.

1 package direct-set buttermilk starter culture or store-bought cultured buttermilk (see Try Instead note that follows)

4 cups whole milk

1. In a jar, mix the buttermilk starter culture into the whole milk.

2. Cover the jar using a clean kitchen towel, and secure it with a rubber band.

3. Place the jar in a warm location, at around 70°F to 77°F, and let it sit for 12 to 24 hours.

4. Once the milk has thickened, put a lid on the jar and transfer it to cold storage.

TRY INSTEAD

To make a version using store-bought cultured buttermilk, reduce the amount of milk in this recipe to 3 cups, and add 1 cup of cultured buttermilk to it. Then follow the same steps outlined in the preceding recipe.

CRÈME FRAÎCHE

MAKES: 1 PINT **PREP TIME:** 5 MINUTES **FERMENTATION TIME:** 12 TO 36 HOURS

BEGINNER

Crème fraîche is yet another relatively inexpensive-to-make item for which gourmet markets charge astronomical amounts. Avoid the high cost and make this simple, creamy treat at home with next to no effort. Spoon the finished product over fresh fruits, pancakes, or pies, or take the savory route and add it to sauces and soups to up their richness.

1 tablespoon cultured buttermilk
2 cups heavy cream

1. Mix the buttermilk and cream together in a jar.

2. Cover the jar with a clean kitchen towel secured with a rubber band, and place it in a warm location ranging from 70°F to 77°F.

3. After 12 hours, check the ferment. If it is thickened and creamy, it is done. If not, leave it to continue fermenting for up to 24 hours more, until a thick consistency is achieved.

4. Place a lid on the jar and transfer it to the refrigerator, where the crème fraîche will continue to thicken. Use within 7 to 10 days.

5

DAIRY

KEFIR CHEESE

MAKES: 1 QUART **PREP TIME:** 5 MINUTES PREP TIME, UP TO 12 HOURS OF RESTING

BEGINNER

Kefir cheese is an incredibly versatile soft cheese that is the epitome of an easy do-it-yourself project. With nothing more than a coffee filter, strainer, and glass jar, you can create this mild, crumbly cheese that can be dressed up in countless ways with savory or sweet seasonings, or simply enjoyed plain. Bonus: You produce whey during this process, which you can store in your refrigerator for future fermenting projects.

2 cups Kefir (page 79)

1. Place a large coffee filter in a large strainer, and then set the strainer over a bowl or jar to collect the whey.

2. Pour the kefir into the coffee filter. Cover the strainer and jar with a clean kitchen towel, and place in your refrigerator overnight.

3. In the morning, remove the kefir cheese from the strainer, and store it in an airtight container in the refrigerator.

4. Reserve the whey in a separate jar, refrigerated, until ready to use.

A CLOSER LOOK

This cheese has a consistency similar to ricotta—it is slightly spreadable, soft, and crumbly. To season it before draining for added flavor, mix the kefir with ½ teaspoon salt and your favorite herbs or ingredients, such as basil, oregano, thyme, parsley, or even puréed sun-dried tomatoes.

YOGURT

MAKES: 1 QUART **PREP TIME**: 10 MINUTES **FERMENTATION TIME**: 12 TO 24 HOURS

INTERMEDIATE

Unlike many other dairy ferments, yogurt requires incubation at a higher temperature, making it a slightly more difficult project. But there are many ways to achieve this temperature at home that don't require fancy equipment. If you happen to have a dehydrator with temperature controls that can maintain 110°F, this is the optimal solution. But a small cooler filled with hot tap water can also maintain a temperature warm enough to produce a delicious yogurt. Alternatively, a small, insulated lunch bag can do the trick when the jar of yogurt is surrounded by a couple of jars filled with piping hot water. Use whatever items you have at home to get a batch of homemade yogurt going—the extra effort will be well worth it.

3¾ cups whole milk
¼ cup yogurt starter

1. Heat the milk in a saucepan until it reaches 180°F. Remove the pan from the heat, and let it cool to 110°F. To speed up the process, immerse the bottom of the pan in an ice water bath.

2. Measure the yogurt starter into a clean quart jar. Once the milk cools to 110°F, pour it into the jar, leaving about 1 inch of headspace. Close the jar and give it a good shake to fully incorporate the starter.

3. Place the jar in your insulated incubator. If there is no heat source, add hot water to a couple of mason jars to keep the yogurt warm. If the incubator has rigid sides, fill it with hot water to just below the jar closures. Close the incubator.

4. The yogurt will be done in 12 to 24 hours. Check after 12 hours for consistency, and if using an incubator with no heat source, add additional hot water to maintain a temperature above 100°F.

A CLOSER LOOK

Once you begin regularly making yogurt, you can use the starter from your most recent batch as the starter for a new batch. At the beginning of your project, however, you can obtain a starter culture from your grocery store. Select a plain, whole-milk yogurt that does not contain additional ingredients, such as gelatin or dry milk powder. To enable it to produce a new batch, yogurt must also contain active cultures. Read labels carefully before making your selection.

5

DAIRY

CULTURED BUTTER

MAKES: ABOUT 1 PINT **PREP TIME**: 5 MINUTES, 15 TO 20 MINUTES AFTER FERMENTATION
FERMENTATION TIME: 12 TO 24 HOURS

INTERMEDIATE

Cultured butter has a rich taste that you just don't get in store-bought butter. Although the process adds extra time to the project of butter making, it is well worth the additional effort for the flavor alone. First, culture the cream used to make butter, and then churn the cream. You will also make true buttermilk, the liquid left over from the butter-making process, which has a signature tang and a thinner, more watery consistency than the fermented version. Save this for future baking projects, as it can be used interchangeably with cultured buttermilk in most recipes. Using a stand mixer, as outlined in this recipe, is the easiest way to churn butter efficiently at home, although it can also be done manually or with a hand mixer.

4 cups heavy cream

¼ cup Kefir (page 79), homemade Yogurt (page 87), or cultured buttermilk

1 cup ice water (plus more if needed), divided

Salt (optional)

Herbs (optional)

1. Pour the cream into a wide-mouth jar, and add whichever type of culture you are using. Mix the two together using a plastic whisk. Cover the jar with a clean kitchen towel held in place with a rubber band. Place in a warm location with a temperature between 70°F and 77°F.

2. Once the cream has thickened slightly and developed a tangy aroma—after about 12 to 24 hours—transfer it to the refrigerator for at least 1 hour to chill.

3. Place a strainer over a bowl or jar, and line it with a few layers of cheesecloth or a couple of coffee filters.

4. Place the cream mixture in the bowl of a stand mixer. Cover the top of the bowl with plastic wrap or a kitchen towel to prevent splashing, and then turn the mixer on at medium-high speed. The cream will begin by foaming and then form into peaks, begin to turn grainy, and finally, the butter and buttermilk will separate. The whole process will take about 5 to 10 minutes.

5. Pour the butter and buttermilk into the set up strainer. Once the buttermilk has stopped dripping, grab the filter or cheesecloth holding the butter solids and squeeze it firmly several times to extract any leftover buttermilk.

6. Place the buttermilk in a separate container with a tightly fitting lid and refrigerate.

7. Clean the bowl from the mixer and add ½ cup ice water to the bowl. Place the butter in the bowl, and press it with a silicone spatula. As you do this, buttermilk is pulled from the butter into the water, and it will become cloudy. Pour the water out and replace it with another ½ cup of fresh ice water. Repeat this process until the water remains clear while pressing the butter. You will notice that the butter becomes firmer as you repeat this step.

8. Sprinkle salt (if using) and herbs (if using) over the butter, and knead them into the butter until evenly mixed throughout.

9. Pack the butter into a lidded glass storage jar. Or, using a piece of wax paper, roll the butter into a log. Cultured butter can be stored in the refrigerator for up to 3 weeks or frozen for several months.

TRY INSTEAD

If you don't have a stand mixer, you can make this the old-fashioned way. Place the cultured milk in a mason jar, and tightly close its lid. Shake the jar vigorously until the butter and buttermilk separate, which may take upward of 20 minutes (and give you a good arm workout in the process!).

CREAM CHEESE

MAKES: 1 QUART PREP TIME: 15 MINUTES, 6 TO 12 HOURS DRAINING TIME
FERMENTATION TIME: 14 TO 16 HOURS

ADVANCED

Homemade cream cheese is a rich, decadent treat. This project involves a few more steps and special ingredients than others in this category, but don't let that put you off—the final product is exquisite. Season your homemade cream cheese with your favorite ingredients, such as minced garden veggies, pickled jalapeños, sun-dried tomatoes, or strawberries for an amazing sweet or savory spread on bagels and sandwiches.

1 quart whole milk

1 quart heavy cream

¼ teaspoon mesophilic aromatic starter culture (see A Closer Look, which follows)

2 drops liquid rennet

2 tablespoons water

¾ teaspoon sea salt

1. Add the milk and cream to a nonreactive saucepan. Heat the milk to 75°F, and then promptly remove it from the heat. Add the culture to the surface of the milk-cream mixture and allow it to dissolve on its own, which should take about 2 to 3 minutes. Once dissolved, thoroughly mix it in using a nonmetal spoon.

2. Combine the rennet and the water, and mix well before adding to the milk mixture. Incorporate the rennet gently by using 2 or 3 up-and-down strokes instead of mixing circularly; it is crucial not to over-mix at this stage.

3. Cover the pot using a clean kitchen towel, and let it stand at room temperature for 14 to 16 hours. At this time, the cheese will look like yogurt, and you may see that the whey is separated from the curds.

4. Place a clean kitchen towel or several layers of cheesecloth in a bowl, and spoon the cheese into it. Gather the sides of the cheesecloth and tie it into a knot around the handle of a long spoon—the utensil can be suspended across the bowl to elevate the cheese and allow the whey to drip out. Leave the cream cheese suspended for 6 to 12 hours, or until it has thickened to the desired consistency.

5. Add the salt to the cheese, and mix in thoroughly in a large bowl or mixer.

6. Store in a mason jar or press it into a brick with wax paper, and refrigerate for up to 2 weeks.

A CLOSER LOOK

Mesophilic starter cultures are the most commonly used type of culture for making low-temperature cheeses. These types of starter cultures work best in dairy products when the temperature is around 86°F. Although mesophilic aromatic starter cultures are widely available, a cream cheese starter culture can be substituted. Cream cheese starter contains rennet, so if you use it, omit the rennet called for in the recipe.

6

GRAINS & BREADS

Traditional bread making relied solely on wild yeasts and a long, slow rise to create a leavened loaf. Pulled from "thin air," these breads can take a couple of days from start to finish, a feat that requires some planning in our modern, schedule-oriented society.

During this process, the natural yeast in the bread ferments the flour, producing carbon dioxide gas, which is responsible for the dough's subsequent rising. Unfortunately for your gut, the beneficial microbes responsible do not survive the baking process. But by creating and cultivating a small starter, you can keep these microbes alive to do their important work on your next batch.

Modern nutrition dictates that whole grains are best. What it does not mention is that our ancestors prepared grains in a different way than we do, usually soaking or fermenting them before cooking. Although our busy schedules have caused us to fall away from this traditional practice, you can bring back this ancient craft in your kitchen with relatively little effort.

All grains contain phytic acid, an anti-nutrient, in their outer layer or bran. When untreated, this phytic acid combines with zinc, iron, phosphorus, and calcium in the intestinal tract and prevents their absorption. Soaking gives lactobacilli bacteria and other organisms present in the atmosphere the opportunity to neutralize much of the phytic acid present in grains before they reach your mouth.

By soaking and sprouting grains, you begin the work of breaking down hard-to-digest carbohydrates and proteins, making the later digestion and absorption of the nutrients in them easier. People with sensitivity to commercially prepared grains and breads sometimes find that soaking and sprouting grains can ease some digestive discomfort and allow them to eat these foods again in a limited way.

This chapter is a sampling of several different types of soaked, sprouted, and wildly fermented grains. The subject is vast, with countless books dedicated to this one aspect of the craft of fermenting. Use these recipes as an introduction to the topic and a way to get you started on this traditional practice. If you find yourself getting seriously intrigued by these foods and the practices behind them, explore the options further with some of the titles listed in the Resources section (page 193) of this book.

For most recipes, no special supplies are needed—just a few jars for soaking and sprouting, and a couple of nonreactive bowls. The one exception is Sprouted Whole Grain Flour (page 98), which requires a dehydrator and a grain mill.

Some recipes call for a yogurt or whey starter culture for soaking, while others, such as sourdough breads, rely solely on wild yeasts. As with other recipes in this book, you can make your own Yogurt (page 87) or whey (page 23), or purchase a commercially made product, such as plain whole fat yogurt, to get started.

SOAKED OATMEAL

MAKES: 4 SERVINGS **PREP TIME:** 5 MINUTES, 10 TO 15 MINUTES COOKING TIME
FERMENTATION TIME: UP TO 24 HOURS

BEGINNER

Soaking oatmeal in a combination of water and fermented dairy before cooking makes it more digestible, not to mention more delicious. Use one of your own dairy ferments for this recipe, or substitute store-bought—just make sure it is unflavored and contains no added preservatives or unnecessary ingredients. Save your leftover soaked oatmeal, and use it the next day to create Oatmeal Pancakes (page 179).

1 cup old-fashioned oats

2 tablespoons fermented dairy product, such as kefir, plain yogurt, buttermilk, or whey (page 23)

2 cups water, divided

½ teaspoon sea salt

1 teaspoon ground cinnamon (optional)

Maple syrup (optional)

1. In a medium nonreactive bowl, mix the oats and fermented dairy. Heat 1 cup of the water on the stove or in the microwave until just lukewarm, and stir into the oat mixture. Cover the bowl with a clean kitchen towel, and leave it in a warm location for at least 7 hours or as long as 24 hours.

2. When you are ready to cook it, first drain the oatmeal mixture. Bring the remaining 1 cup water to a boil in a small pot. Add the salt and the drained oatmeal mixture. Reduce the heat and cover the pot. Simmer for 10 minutes, stirring occasionally. Add more water to thin the oatmeal, if desired.

3. Add the cinnamon (if using) and maple syrup (if using) to sweeten. Serve.

A CLOSER LOOK

Limit sugar consumption for good health and to maintain weight. When you use sweeteners, do so in nutrient-dense foods, such as oatmeal, where you are getting plenty of nutritional value along with the added sugar.

SOAKED BUTTERMILK PANCAKES

MAKES: 8 TO 12 PANCAKES PREP TIME: 5 MINUTES, 10 MINUTES COOKING TIME
FERMENTATION TIME: 12 HOURS BAKE TIME: 15 MINUTES

BEGINNER

If the idea of soaking your breakfast the day or night before sounds discouraging, consider this: It is actually a great tool to help you plan meals. By simply mixing flour and yogurt ahead of time, you are ensuring a nutritious and delicious meal for you and your family the next day. It takes the rush out of mornings, and everyone will be so happy you made the extra effort when they see beautifully fluffy, piping hot pancakes on the table. Instead of buttermilk, these pancakes can be made with any similar soured dairy ferment, such as yogurt or kefir.

1 cup whole wheat flour

1 cup buckwheat flour

2 cups buttermilk, yogurt, or kefir

½ teaspoon sea salt

2 teaspoons baking soda

2 tablespoons melted butter

2 eggs

1. Add the flours and the buttermilk, yogurt, or kefir to a nonreactive bowl. Stir well and cover with a clean kitchen towel. Let sit at room temperature overnight, or for about 12 hours.

2. When ready to make the pancakes, add all the additional ingredients and mix to combine.

3. Spoon the batter onto a hot griddle or skillet, using about ¼ cup of batter for each pancake. When tiny bubbles appear on the top of each pancake, flip it over and cook until completely cooked through. Continue and repeat until you have used all of the batter.

A CLOSER LOOK

Buckwheat is not a true wheat but is actually the seed of a fruit related to sorrel and rhubarb. Buckwheat is high in flavonoids, and people who eat a lot of buckwheat are less likely to develop elevated cholesterol or elevated blood pressure. Buckwheat also supports blood sugar control better than other grains. For gluten-sensitive individuals, it is a great alternative to wheat. If you are on a gluten-free diet, substitute buckwheat for the whole wheat flour in this recipe.

SOAKED OATMEAL MUFFINS

MAKES: 1 DOZEN **PREP TIME:** 5 MINUTES, 10 MINUTES THE NEXT DAY
FERMENTATION TIME: 12 TO 24 HOURS

BEGINNER

This is a super simple recipe for hearty oat muffins that you can use as a springboard to wherever your taste buds take you. Add fresh or dried fruits, nuts, chocolate chips, or anything else you like to create a nutritious breakfast or snack. Soaking the flour first adds a noticeable and welcome tang to these easily customizable treats.

2 cups whole wheat flour

1 cup old-fashioned oats

2 cups kefir or yogurt

⅔ cup honey

3 eggs

4 tablespoons melted coconut oil

2 teaspoons baking soda

½ teaspoon baking powder

¼ teaspoon sea salt

1. Combine the whole wheat flour, oats, and kefir or yogurt in a nonreactive bowl and mix well. Cover with a clean kitchen towel, and leave in a warm location for 12 to 24 hours.

2. When you are ready to bake the muffins, preheat your oven to 375°F. Line a muffin tin with paper muffin cups, or grease each muffin cup individually.

3. Add all the additional ingredients to the fermented flour mixture and stir to combine. Spoon the batter into the muffin cups. Bake for 15 minutes. Use a toothpick inserted into a muffin to check for doneness. If it comes out clean, the muffins are done.

6

GRAINS & BREADS

SPROUTED WHOLE-GRAIN FLOUR

MAKES: 1 POUND **PREP TIME:** 5 MINUTES, 5 MINUTES DAILY **FERMENTATION TIME:** 3 TO 4 DAYS

INTERMEDIATE

Sprouting grains produces a slightly sweeter flour, and releases many of its antinutrients, so that your body is better able to digest the nutrients in the flour. Although sprouting grains is a simple process, turning them into flour is another process altogether, one that is time-consuming. But completing this task, which has deep historical roots, is the way that many people eat grains to get greater health benefits and fewer side effects. You will need a dehydrator and a grain mill to make this recipe, but once you get started, your gut and your palate will thank you.

1 pound wheat berries or other whole grain (spelt berries, einkorn berries, rice)

Water

1 tablespoon vinegar

1. Place the wheat berries or other grain in a large bowl, and cover with 2 inches of water. Add the vinegar. Cover and place in a warm location for 12 to 24 hours.

2. Pour the wheat berries into a colander to drain. Rinse them well with cold water, stirring them with your clean hands as you go. Leave them to drain in the colander, placed over a bowl. Then, 2 or 3 times a day, rinse the grains again and allow them to drain. Continue this process for 2 to 3 more days, until a tiny sprout emerges from the grains. They are ready to use when roughly 50 percent of the grains have sprouted.

3. Transfer the grains to a dehydrator lined with nonstick baking sheets, and dry the grains for 12 to 18 hours at 115°F, or until firm.

4. Grind the grains into a fine flour, and store it in the freezer until you are ready to use it.

TRY INSTEAD

If you don't have the equipment or time to sprout your own flour, don't worry. There are some other options if you want to add this healthy alternative to your diet. Check health food stores in your area, as sprouted flour is becoming more widely available. If you can't source it from a local shop, consider buying it online, where you will have a larger selection of quality products.

SPROUTED CHOCOLATE ZUCCHINI BREAD

MAKES: 2 LOAVES **PREP TIME:** 15 MINUTES **BAKE TIME:** 55 MINUTES

INTERMEDIATE

Increase the nutritional value of this traditional vegetable loaf by using a sprouted whole wheat version of Sprouted Whole-Grain Flour (page 98) instead of the usual white flour. Adding cocoa powder to the bread is an appealing and tasty tweak and ensures that none of the bread will go to waste. If you have a bumper crop of zucchini, bake several loaves at once and freeze, as zucchini bread stores exceedingly well.

3 cups sprouted whole wheat flour

¼ cup cocoa powder

1 tablespoon ground cinnamon

1 teaspoon baking soda

½ teaspoon baking powder

1 teaspoon sea salt

¾ cup sugar

¾ cup honey

3 eggs

1 cup coconut oil, melted

2 teaspoons vanilla

2 cups shredded zucchini

1. Preheat an oven to 350°F, and grease and flour two 9-by-5-inch loaf pans.

2. Mix the sprouted whole wheat flour, cocoa powder, cinnamon, baking soda, baking powder, and salt together in a bowl and set aside.

3. In another bowl, mix all the remaining ingredients together. Pour the wet ingredients into the bowl with the flour mixture, and stir well until no dry ingredients are visible.

4. Pour the batter into the prepared pans, and place them in the hot oven. Bake for 55 minutes, or until a toothpick inserted in the center of the bread comes out clean.

A CLOSER LOOK

If you don't plan on eating both loaves in 3 to 5 days, freeze one to save for later. Wrap it first tightly in plastic wrap, and then cover it in a layer of aluminum foil. Frozen, the zucchini bread will keep for several months. When you are ready to eat it, leave it on the counter overnight to defrost.

SOURDOUGH STARTER

MAKES: 1½ CUPS **PREP TIME:** 5 MINUTES, 10 MINUTES DAILY **FERMENTATION TIME:** ABOUT 6 DAYS

INTERMEDIATE

Sourdough starter provides both the leavening action and the flavor in the well-known, slightly tangy sourdough bread. Created with just flour, water, and time, this mixture is nourished by the yeasts in the atmosphere. The starter takes on a life of its own over the course of several days to become a bubbly, growing mass. It may seem like a lot of work to continually add more flour to "feed" the starter, but after you gain a little experience, it will take just a couple of minutes. Once you get it going and take proper care of it, your sourdough starter can continue to inoculate future batches and create many delicious baked items in its lifetime.

1 cup whole wheat flour
8 cups unbleached all-purpose flour, divided
4½ cups water, divided, at room temperature

1. Add 1 cup whole wheat flour to a glass quart jar. Add ½ cup water. Stir this mixture together and cover with a clean kitchen towel. Place in a warm (70°F) location for 24 hours.

2. Discard half of the starter. Add 1 cup unbleached all-purpose flour to the starter, along with another ½ cup water. Stir again until all the flour is incorporated and cover again. Allow to rest for 24 hours.

3. On days 3 to 5, you will feed the starter twice a day. To do this, measure a heaping ½ cup of the starter and reserve. Discard the remaining starter. Add 1 cup of unbleached all-purpose flour and ½ cup water to the measured starter. Stir and cover with a kitchen towel for 12 hours, and repeat this process twice daily through the fifth day.

4. When the starter doubles in size between 12-hour feedings, it is ready to go. At this time, it will have developed a tangy, pleasing aroma. Finish it off with a final feeding of 1 cup unbleached all-purpose flour and ½ cup water, and allow it to rest, covered, for another 6 to 8 hours.

5. At this point, the starter is ready to be used in your favorite recipes, and you may measure off the amount you need, up to 8 ounces. Transfer the remaining starter, which will be about 4 ounces (or ½ cup) to another container for storage. If you plan on making bread regularly, continue to feed it daily.

A CLOSER LOOK

If you don't plan on baking daily, that's okay. Simply place the starter in the refrigerator, covered, for up to 6 months at a time. Before using again, return it to room temperature, discard half of it, and continue to feed it for 3 days before using it again.

WHY THE WASTE?

You may be wondering why on earth the sourdough starter recipe requires you to toss out so much. Two reasons: The first is that it keeps the volume from getting way too big, which otherwise becomes unmanageable after just a few days. The second is that by keeping the volume down, active yeast in the starter has more food to eat, making it better able to thrive and grow. If you didn't discard half, not only would you have a huge amount of starter, but the yeasts would be competing against many other yeasts for food, leaving some unable to multiply.

NO-KNEAD WHOLE-GRAIN SOURDOUGH BREAD

MAKES: 1 LOAF **PREP TIME:** 15 MINUTES, 28 HOURS RESTING
FERMENTATION TIME: 10 HOURS **BAKE TIME:** 55 MINUTES

INTERMEDIATE

No-knead breads are simple and take the most arduous step out of bread making. Not only do they require little work, they really do compare to bakery breads in terms of quality and flavor. Create this artisan-style loaf in your home with little work, and your family will quickly ask for more.

1 cup Sourdough Starter (page 100)

2 cups water, room temperature

2 cups whole wheat flour or the whole wheat version of Sprouted Whole-Grain Flour (page 98)

4 cups unbleached all-purpose flour

2½ teaspoons salt

1. In a glass or ceramic bowl, add the sourdough starter and water, and mix together well. Add the whole wheat flour and mix again, then add the unbleached flour and salt, mixing again until all the flour is incorporated.

2. Cover the bowl with a clean kitchen towel, and let it sit on the counter for 6 to 8 hours. Then refrigerate the dough for 24 hours.

3. Place the bowl back on the counter and allow it to warm up for 1 to 2 hours.

4. Lightly flour a work surface and turn out the dough. Fold the dough over itself 3 to 6 times.

5. Place the dough in a clean bowl, cover with a kitchen towel, and leave at room temperature for 2 hours.

6. Preheat the oven and a cast iron Dutch oven with a lid to 450°F for 30 minutes. Remove the Dutch oven from the hot oven carefully, wearing oven mitts. Lower the dough into the pan, return the lid, and place it in the oven. Bake for 35 minutes.

7. Remove the lid of the Dutch oven, and lower the temperature to 400°F. Bake for an additional 20 minutes.

8. Remove the pot from the oven, and transfer the bread to a cooling rack by carefully inverting it. Let the bread rest for 45 minutes before serving.

MULTIGRAIN SOURDOUGH BREAD

MAKES: 1 LOAF **PREP TIME**: 15 MINUTES, ABOUT 4 HOURS RESTING
FERMENTATION TIME: 24 HOURS **BAKE TIME**: 70 MINUTES

INTERMEDIATE

Sometimes you want a bread with a little more oomph—a little extra flavor and chewiness—and this is that bread. Loaded with whole grains and a mixture of rye, whole wheat, and white flours, this bread is packed with both flavor and nutrition. Enjoy a piece as toast, spread with jam, for a wake-you-up breakfast treat, or serve it alongside your favorite soup or salad.

⅔ cup buckwheat groats

⅔ cup rye berries

1⅔ cups Sourdough Starter (page 100)

1½ cups water

1 cup rye flour

1 cup whole wheat flour

1¾ cups unbleached all-purpose flour

1¾ cups bread flour

2 tablespoons chia seeds

2 teaspoons sea salt

2 tablespoons honey

1. The day before making the bread, place the buckwheat groats and rye berries in a 1-quart mason jar. Bring a pot of water to boil, and pour it into the jar, covering the mixture by a few inches. Leave on the counter for 24 hours, replacing the water with fresh, cool water twice during that period.

2. The following day, add all the ingredients to a bowl, except the salt and honey, and mix until everything is well incorporated. Cover the dough with a clean kitchen towel, and let it rest for 40 minutes.

3. Add the salt and honey to the dough and mix well again. Cover and let it rest for 30 more minutes.

4. Fold the dough over itself several times, cover it again, and let it rest for a final 30 minutes.

5. Line a large bread pan with parchment paper, and place the dough in it, stretching it as needed to fit the pan. Cover with a clean, wet kitchen towel, and let it rest until it reaches the top of the pan, or about 2 hours in a 70°F kitchen.

6. Preheat the oven to 350°F and bake the bread for 70 minutes, or until its crust is well browned.

A CLOSER LOOK

Chia seeds are nutritional powerhouses. Packed with omega-3 fatty acids, carbohydrates, protein, fiber, antioxidants, and calcium, they are a nutrient-dense superfood.

SOURDOUGH BAGUETTES

MAKES: 2 BAGUETTES **PREP TIME:** 15 MINUTES, 16 TO 28 HOURS RESTING
FERMENTATION TIME: 24 HOURS **BAKE TIME:** 30 MINUTES

ADVANCED

Baguettes may seem like an out-of-reach baking project, but really, they are not all that tricky for the home baker to master. Using just a sourdough starter for leavening, these loaves are wonderfully airy on the inside and still have that characteristic sourdough tang. Considered a demi-baguette—as opposed to a true baguette, which would measure at least 26 inches in length—this crusty, French-inspired masterpiece will fit inside a standard home oven for easy baking.

½ cup Sourdough Starter (page 100)
1½ cups whole wheat flour
1 cup unbleached all-purpose flour
⅞ cup water
1 teaspoon sea salt
Flour, for dusting

1. Mix the sourdough starter, flours, and water together in a bowl by hand or using a stand mixer. Allow the mixture to rest for 20 to 40 minutes.

2. Add the salt and knead by hand or using the dough hook of a stand mixer for 5 minutes.

3. Cover the bowl with a clean towel, and allow it to rest for 1 hour. Then fold the dough over itself 10 to 12 times, re-cover, and let rest again for another hour. Fold the dough again 10 to 12 more times.

4. Transfer the dough to a new bowl. Cover the bowl with a generous piece of plastic wrap, and then push the plastic wrap down so that it is snug around the dough, forming a nearly airtight seal. Place the bowl in the refrigerator for 12 to 24 hours.

5. Take the dough from the refrigerator, and remove the plastic wrap. Cover the bowl with a kitchen towel, and leave the dough on the counter for about 1 hour to allow it to come to room temperature.

6. Place a baking stone in your oven, and preheat it to 500°F for 30 minutes.

7. Turn the dough on to a clean, well-floured surface. Divide the dough into two equal pieces. Shape each piece into a long, thin log by gathering it together and rolling it out gently with your hands. Allow it to rest on the counter for 5 to 10 minutes.

8. Roll each log again to elongate it, taking care to not make it longer than your baking stone. Cover the loaves with a clean kitchen towel while the oven heats.

9. Bring a pot of water to boil on the stove. Place a rimmed baking sheet in the oven, below the baking stone, and carefully pour the boiling water into the baking sheet during the last couple of minutes of preheating. This creates steam, which is important for making a good, crunchy crust.

10. Using a sharp knife, slash the tops of the baguettes with 3 lines at a 45° angle, place them on the baking stone, and quickly close the oven to prevent the steam from escaping.

11. Bake for 20 to 25 minutes, or until well browned.

12. Transfer to a cooling rack, and let rest for 30 minutes before slicing.

TRY INSTEAD

If you don't have a baking stone, you can use a standard baking sheet to make these baguettes. Although a baking stone retains more heat and creates a crisper crust, you can also have perfectly good results using any type of baking sheet lined with a piece of parchment paper to prevent sticking.

NAAN

MAKES: 6 BREADS **PREP TIME**: 15 MINUTES, 4 HOURS RESTING
FERMENTATION TIME: 12 TO 36 HOURS

ADVANCED

Naan, just one of countless flat breads produced in India, has been popularized by its constant place on Indian restaurant menus across the world. Soft and silky, this bread is a perfect accompaniment to a number of curries, meats, and other wet dishes, where it can be used as much as a utensil to soak up fragrant, spicy juices as it is a side dish. Depending on your kitchen temperature, the starter for this will need to be fermented for 12 to 36 hours, with more time in the cooler months and less in the warmer ones. If you are able to prepare homemade ghee for spreading on these while you wait for fermentation to take place, you will be extremely glad you did.

2½ cups spelt flour, divided

2 teaspoons sugar, divided

½ cup water

½ cup milk

1½ tablespoons melted ghee or butter, plus more for brushing

¾ teaspoon salt

1 teaspoon baking powder

1. Add ½ cup of spelt flour, 1 teaspoon of sugar, and the water to a small jar. Cover with a clean cloth, and place in a warm area in your kitchen. Leave for 12 to 36 hours, or until it is bubbly and fermentation is visible.

2. Pour the milk, ghee, salt, and remaining 1 teaspoon sugar into a bowl. Add the starter and mix well.

3. In a separate bowl, combine the baking powder and the remaining 2 cups of flour and mix well. Slowly pour the flour mixture into the bowl, and mix to incorporate it. Knead with your hands until you form a smooth dough that naturally pulls away from the sides of the bowl. If the dough is not achieving the proper consistency, add a bit more flour until you have a soft dough that is a bit sticky but not so sticky that it gets all over your hands.

4. Grease a bowl with oil or ghee, and place the dough in it. Cover with plastic wrap. Leave on the counter in a draft-free location for about 4 hours.

5. Preheat the oven to the highest temperature possible, typically around 500°F for most home ovens. Place a large baking stone or sheet in the oven.

6. Place the dough on a lightly floured work surface, and divide it into 6 equal portions. Using a rolling pin or your hands, shape each round into a flat, circular, or oval piece roughly ¼-inch thick.

7. When the oven is ready, open it and place 2 or more pieces in the oven, depending on the size of your baking stone or sheet. Bake for 1 to 2 minutes on each side, or until they are well browned and you see charred spots on both sides.

8. Remove the naan from the oven with a spatula, and repeat until all of them are baked. Brush the breads with melted ghee, and place them inside a piece of aluminum foil, with the top folded over to keep them warm, until you are finished baking all of the dough. Serve immediately.

7

LEGUMES

The fermentation of legumes has its roots in traditional Asian cultures. Japanese cuisine makes ready use of some of the prime ferments from this category with its ubiquitous use of soy sauce, tofu, and miso. All made from the humble soybean, these products are the base of an almost infinite number of flavorings and foods prepared throughout the country. In Indian cuisine, a combination of lentils and rice is fermented to create the South Indian breakfast staple dosa, a soured, fried crêpe-like dish.

Though popular choices, soybeans and lentils are not the only legumes with the ability to be transformed. Other varieties can be soaked, sprouted, and fermented in similar ways to increase their nutritional value and ease digestibility. These preparation methods are used to create the soured lentils, hummus, and black bean dip in this book, though their use in your kitchen is practically limitless once you learn the basic process.

Legumes are an entire family of seedpods, which include peas, beans, lentils, soybeans, and peanuts. These plant foods are packed with vitamins and minerals, and are high in protein and healthy omega-3 and omega-6 fatty acids. Because of their dense nutritional content, they are an integral part of any healthy diet. According to Joel Fuhrman, MD, a *New York Times* best-selling author, family physician, and internationally recognized expert on nutrition and natural healing (see References, page 194), the regular consumption of legumes can help you manage weight, prevent diabetes, and protect the body against colon cancer and other cancers.

Legumes are packed with fiber and resistant starches, which are carbohydrates that cannot be broken down in the digestive tract. These starches limit the amount of calories absorbed by the body while satiating hunger, reduce spikes in blood sugar after eating, and, perhaps most notably, act as food for organisms in the gut to ferment into anticancer compounds.

Although their health benefits are innumerable, perhaps the most wonderful thing about this food group is its versatility. Legumes can be transformed into soups, salads, stews, or spreads, and they readily take on any spices and seasonings with which they are flavored; they can even be ground into flour for use in some creative (and gluten-free) baking projects.

With all these benefits, the downside is that eating legumes, in large quantities especially, can lead to digestive distress, particularly when they are prepared improperly. Soaking legumes before cooking can help prevent this discomfort, and fermenting them can help even more. By beginning to break the legumes down, this process can be the key to preventing ill effects, such as bloating and gas, which so many people experience after eating legumes.

As with grains, fermenting legumes requires little equipment to get started. Once you get into more complex projects, such as soy sauce, miso, or natto, you will need to purchase starter cultures to ensure the correct bacteria takes hold. When you are just starting out, though, all you need is a bowl or jar and a little extra time to soak or sprout your legumes to the point of better digestibility.

SOURED LENTILS

MAKES: 4 CUPS **PREP TIME**: 10 MINUTES **FERMENTATION TIME**: 24 TO 48 HOURS

BEGINNER

By fermenting lentils before cooking, you minimize their phytic acid and other hard-to-digest starches. You also add flavor and afford them an even quicker cooking time. This is one of the simplest legume projects in this book and a perfect one to start with. Try these Soured Lentils in our Lentil Soup (page 182), or use them in any of your favorite, go-to lentil dishes for a slightly different, appealing flavor.

2 cups lentils
Water for soaking
½ to 1 cup whey, yogurt, or kefir

1. Add the lentils to a nonreactive bowl, and cover them with lukewarm water. Add ¼ of the whey, yogurt, or kefir, and mix well to incorporate. Cover with a clean kitchen towel, and keep the jar at room temperature for 12 hours.

2. After 12 hours, drain the lentils and repeat the process, adding water and ¼ of the whey, yogurt, or kefir to them. Depending on the temperature in your home, it will take 24 to 48 hours to complete the fermentation process.

3. Drain and rinse the lentils. Cook as specified in your chosen recipe.

7

LEGUMES

SPROUTED HUMMUS

MAKES: 2 CUPS **PREP TIME:** 10 MINUTES **SPROUTING TIME:** 3 TO 5 DAYS

BEGINNER

Soaking produces the most noticeable results in a dish in which this practice is traditional, such as hummus, which nowadays is typically made using cooked chickpeas. In this recipe, however, cooking is omitted, and after 3 to 5 days of soaking, the chickpeas sprout, growing about a 1/8-inch tail. Because soaking removes antinutrients and enzyme inhibitors that would block absorption of nutrients, this is a healthy way to get the heaviest dose of vitamins and minerals from this dish.

2 cups chickpeas

2 tablespoons freshly squeezed lemon juice

4 tablespoons tahini paste

1/3 cup olive oil, plus more for garnish

4 garlic cloves (use Fermented Garlic [page 150], if desired)

1 teaspoon sea salt

1/4 teaspoon ground cumin

4 tablespoons water

1. Cover the chickpeas with water, and soak overnight for at least 12 hours.

2. The following day, rinse the chickpeas. Leave to drain in a colander covered by a clean kitchen towel, which will prevent debris and insects from getting into the legumes.

3. Later in the day, rinse the chickpeas again. In warm weather, the chickpeas will need to be rinsed 3 or more times a day, but if the weather is cool, twice a day is sufficient. The chickpeas should remain damp between rinsing.

4. Continue this process for 3 to 5 days, until the chickpeas have sprouted. Do not allow the sprouts to grow longer than 1/4 inch, as they will begin to impart a bitter taste. Don't worry if not all the chickpeas sprout—when at least 50 percent have sprouted, you can proceed with the recipe. Pick through the chickpeas, discarding any that have gone bad.

5. Combine the chickpeas, lemon juice, tahini, olive oil, garlic, salt, and cumin in the bowl of a food processor and process until smooth.

6. Add 2 tablespoons of the water and process again. Add the remaining 2 tablespoons water and continue to process until the hummus becomes uniform in texture.

7. Adjust seasonings as desired, and serve garnished with additional olive oil.

LEGUMES

7

SPROUTED BLACK BEAN DIP

MAKES: 4 CUPS **PREP TIME:** 10 MINUTES **SPROUTING TIME:** 2 TO 6 DAYS
COOK TIME: 12 TO 20 MINUTES

BEGINNER

Sprouting can transform your food. Not only does it significantly shorten cooking time for your favorite black bean dishes, but it also reduces some of their most notable side effects, such as excessive bloating. This Southwestern-themed dip is a fantastic way to get started eating sprouted legumes. Spoon it on tortilla chips for a quick snack, or roll it up in a large lettuce leaf for a gluten-free wrap.

2 cups black beans
2 small tomatoes
1 small onion
1 teaspoon ground cumin
⅛ teaspoon cayenne
2 garlic cloves

1. Cover the black beans in about 2 inches of water, and soak overnight, for at least 12 hours.

2. The following day, rinse the beans and leave them to drain in a colander. Cover the colander with a clean kitchen towel between soakings to prevent debris and insects from getting into the beans.

3. Rinse them again the same day. In warm weather, rinse the beans more than twice a day; in cool weather, twice will suffice. The beans should remain damp between rinsings.

4. Continue this process for the following 2 to 6 days, or until about 50 percent of the beans have sprouted ¼-inch-long shoots.

5. Rinse the beans a final time, and allow them to drain well.

6. Place the sprouted beans in a medium saucepan, and cover with 2 to 3 inches of water. Bring to a boil and simmer for 12 to 20 minutes, or until the beans are tender.

7. Combine the cooked beans with the remaining ingredients in a food processor or blender, and process until a smooth consistency is achieved.

SPROUTED FALAFEL

Falafel is a classic vegetarian sandwich filler that is both flavorful and loaded with nutrition and fiber to keep you full all afternoon long. By sprouting the chickpeas, you can enjoy this iconic Middle Eastern delight without cooking them, while still creating a falafel with the same meaty yet smooth texture. Fry the falafel balls in a bit of oil, and serve them in a piece of pita bread or other flat bread, topped with lettuce, tomato, and a bit of tahini sauce for an easy, nutritious meal.

FOR THE FALAFEL
1 cup chickpeas
1 onion
1 garlic clove
1½ teaspoons sea salt
1 teaspoon baking powder
1 teaspoon freshly squeezed lemon juice
1 teaspoon coriander seeds
2 teaspoons cumin seeds
½ teaspoon cayenne
½ bunch parsley, chopped
4 or 5 sprigs cilantro, chopped
Canola oil, for frying

FOR THE TAHINI SAUCE
2 tablespoons Yogurt (page 87)
1 tablespoon freshly squeezed lemon juice
1 tablespoon tahini
2 tablespoons water
⅛ teaspoon salt

LEGUMES

7

1. Cover the chickpeas in water by about 2 inches, and leave for about 12 hours to soak.

2. The following day, rinse the chickpeas and leave to drain in a colander. Cover the colander with a clean kitchen towel to prevent debris and insects from getting into the legumes.

3. Later in the day, rinse the chickpeas again. In warm weather, the chickpeas will need to be rinsed 3 or more times a day, while in cool weather, 2 times a day is sufficient. The chickpeas should remain damp between rinsings.

4. Continue this process for 2 to 5 days, until about 50 percent of the chickpeas have sprouted and have shoots no longer than ¼ inch. Pick through them, discarding any that have gone bad.

5. In a blender or food processor, combine the chickpeas, onion, garlic, and salt. Process to combine into a paste. Add the baking powder, lemon juice, coriander, cumin, and cayenne, and process until combined. Transfer the mixture to a bowl, and stir in the chopped parsley and cilantro.

6. Divide the mixture into balls the size of golf balls, slightly flattening each one after it is formed. Place the falafel patties on a clean plate in the refrigerator for at least 30 minutes, or as long as overnight before frying.

7. In a large frying pan, heat enough canola oil to just cover its surface. Fry each falafel patty, flipping once, until they are browned on both sides. Drain excess oil on paper towels.

8. Prepare the tahini sauce by combining all the ingredients in a blender until thoroughly combined, and serve with the falafel patties in a pita, garnished with vegetables.

DOSA

MAKES: 6 TO 8 DOSAS **PREP TIME:** 30 MINUTES, 5 HOURS SOAKING TIME
FERMENTATION TIME: 8 HOURS

INTERMEDIATE

Similar to a crêpe, the dosa is a South Indian staple that consists of fermented lentils and rice. Typically served at *dhabas*, or roadside restaurants, dosas are highly versatile, as they can be stuffed with vegetable curries or dipped into a number of sauces—ranging from sambar, a tangy lentil soup with vegetables, to chutneys that are sweet and piquant at the same time. However you serve them, dosas are teeming with flavor and work well served for breakfast or as a midday meal. Try our Masala Dosa on page (189) to experience the king of all dosas, or try simply dipping this version in Coconut Chutney (page 149) or Mint Chutney (page 148) for a filling snack.

½ cup split black lentils, without skin
1 cup rice
1 teaspoon fenugreek seeds
1 cup flattened rice (see A Closer Look, which follows)
1 teaspoon salt
Vegetable oil, for frying

1. Soak the lentils, standard rice, and fenugreek seeds together in a bowl covered by 2 to 3 inches of water for about 5 hours. Drain and set aside.

2. In a separate bowl, add the flattened rice and cover with water. Soak for 5 minutes, drain, and squeeze to get rid of any excess liquid.

3. Put the rice-lentil mixture into a blender and process until smooth. Add the squeezed, flattened rice and continue to process until smooth. Add water as needed to create a thin batter, with a consistency similar to pancake batter.

4. Pour the batter into a bowl and add the salt, stirring well to incorporate.

5. Cover the bowl with a clean kitchen towel, and keep the bowl at room temperature for at least 8 hours, or overnight.

6. Heat a large skillet over medium-high heat. Add oil to the pan to lightly coat. Stir the batter to remix it and, using a ladle, spoon a scant ¼ cup into the hot pan. Immediately, before the batter has a chance to cook through, use the back of the ladle to spread the batter around the bottom of the pan. Drizzle a little extra oil around the edges of the dosa. Cook for about 1 minute, until browned, and then flip it and cook 1 more minute on the second side.

7. Continue cooking the rest of the batter in the same way. Fill the finished dosas with masala curry or pair with chutney to serve.

A CLOSER LOOK

Because this is a dish unique to India, some of the ingredients used in it are not commonly available in Western grocery stores. But these items can be sourced from an Indian grocer or online. See our Resources section on page (193) for sources, and be sure not to skip over certain items. Fenugreek seeds aid the fermentation process and provide a distinctive flavor to the final product. Flattened rice, or *poha*, lends softness to the finished dish.

MISO

MAKES: 1 QUART **PREP TIME**: 15 MINUTES, 3 TO 4 HOURS COOKING
FERMENTATION TIME: 6 MONTHS TO 1 YEAR

INTERMEDIATE

The most difficult thing about making miso is the wait. It will take you anywhere from 6 months to 1 year for this seasoning paste to fully ferment, but when it is done, you will have a uniquely tasty item to brighten your cooking, ready for use in sauces, glazes, marinades, and dressings. This all-purpose ingredient, a cornerstone of Japanese cuisine, uses Aspergillus oryzae—inoculated barley and soybeans, known as koji, to create a one-of-a-kind homemade masterpiece. For best results, weigh all of the ingredients here.

7 ounces dried soybeans
2½ ounces salt, divided
5 ounces dried barley koji

1. Soak the soybeans in double their volume of water for 3 hours. Drain the water.

2. Cover the soybeans with fresh water, bring the water to a boil, reduce the heat to simmer, and cover the soybeans to cook for 3 or 4 hours, or until soft. Drain the beans in a colander, saving the soaking water in a bowl beneath.

3. While they are still hot, mash the soybeans with a potato masher until a smooth consistency is achieved.

4. When the beans cool to a temperature between 95°F and 104°F, it is time to inoculate them. Dissolve 1½ ounces of the salt into ½ cup of the reserved cooking water, and slowly pour this mixture into the beans; crumple the koji into them as well. Using clean hands, mix the mashed beans, koji, and liquid together until a paste forms.

5. Put the paste into a large glass jar for fermentation, and pack it down well to eliminate any air pockets. Sprinkle the remaining 1 ounce of salt over the surface of the miso.

7

LEGUMES

6. Cover the miso using a piece of plastic wrap inserted into the mouth of the container so that it sits directly on the surface of the paste. Add a weight to the top to apply about 1 pound of pressure. Cover with a clean towel, and store in a cool, dark location for 6 months to 1 year.

7. Once finished, divide the miso into smaller containers, cover with tight lids, and store for up to 1 year in the refrigerator.

A CLOSER LOOK

Miso takes from 6 months to 12 months to age properly. For a shorter ferment, begin the miso in spring, when ambient temperatures begin to rise. Longer fermentations can be started in the fall and last until the following fall. During this time, you will see the liquid rise, which is normal. If no liquid is rising, increase the weight applied to the miso. Checking the fermentation can affect the quality, so avoid checking the miso more than once every 2 months.

TEMPEH

MAKES: 2 TEMPEH CAKES **PREP TIME**: 25 MINUTES, 12 HOURS SOAKING, 1 HOUR COOKING
FERMENTATION TIME: 24 TO 48 HOURS

INTERMEDIATE

Tempeh, a fermented soybean cake originating in Indonesia, is a popular choice among vegetarians. A valuable source of protein, it can be added to soups, stews, stir-fries, and other dishes to increase flavor and provide an alternative to meat. Although making your own tempeh takes a bit of work, it also has great rewards. Fresh homemade tempeh has a strong nutty flavor lacking in commercial brands.

2½ cups dried soybeans
2 tablespoons white vinegar
Tempeh starter culture

1. Cover the beans in several inches of water and soak overnight.

2. Dehull the beans by pressing them with a potato masher to split their skins. Remove as many as you can. Removing as many skins as possible allows fermentation to take place, but letting a few remain will not cause a problem.

3. Transfer the beans to a pot, and cover them with fresh water. Cook the beans for about 1 hour, or until soft but not mushy.

4. Transfer the beans to a colander and drain. Spread the beans on a clean kitchen towel and pat dry. Let stand until they are cool to the touch.

5. While the beans are cooling, prepare two 1-gallon plastic zippered storage bags by poking them with holes to allow air to circulate. The beans will ferment inside these bags.

6. Once the beans are cool, transfer them to a large bowl, and add the vinegar, mixing well. Sprinkle the tempeh starter culture over the beans, and thoroughly mix for about 1 minute to ensure it is evenly distributed.

7. Divide the beans evenly between the two prepared bags; flatten and zip them up or seal them.

8. Place the beans in an oven with the pilot light on or a dehydrator set to between 85°F and 90°F for 24 to 48 hours. Check the tempeh every 12 hours. After the first 12 hours, a visible white layer will appear. Between the 24- and 48-hour mark, the beans will be bound together into a cake. At this point, remove them from the incubator, and place them in an airtight storage container. Refrigerate for up to 1 week or freeze for 3 months.

TROUBLESHOOTING

While making tempeh, black or gray spots may form on its surface. This is perfectly normal and not a sign of spoilage. But if there are any odors that seem "off," or if the tempeh develops a slimy or mushy consistency, it should be tossed out.

LEGUMES

7

FERMENTED TOFU

MAKES: 1 BLOCK OF FERMENTED TOFU **PREP TIME:** 10 MINUTES, 15 MINUTES DRAINING
FERMENTATION TIME: 3 TO 5 DAYS, 5 TO 8 WEEKS

INTERMEDIATE

Fermented tofu, or vegan cheese, is made using a traditional preserving process that extends the life of tofu. Creating a pungent yet complexly delicious new soybean food, the process is simple. Have some cheesecloth on hand, and be sure to select extra-firm tofu, as no other type will hold up throughout this process. Use fermented tofu in a stir-fry, spread it on a piece of bread, or eat it on its own as a snack and enjoy its multilayered flavors.

1 **extra-firm block of tofu**
⅔ **cup white miso**
¼ **cup sake**
4 **tablespoons mirin (Japanese rice wine)**

1. Cut the tofu into 2 even pieces. Set the pieces on a clean, dry kitchen towel to drain for about 15 minutes.

2. Combine the miso, sake, and mirin in a small bowl.

3. Select a lidded container that will hold both pieces of tofu in a single layer. Spread ⅓ of the miso mixture into the bottom of the container.

4. Place the cheesecloth on top of the miso mixture, and then place the tofu on top of it. Wrap the cheesecloth around each piece of tofu. Spread the remaining miso mixture on the tops and sides of the tofu.

5. Cover the container and store in the refrigerator for 3 to 5 days. Check daily and pour off any water that accumulates in the container.

6. Line another container with parchment paper. Remove the cheesecloth from the tofu, and transfer the tofu to this container. Cover and refrigerate for 5 to 8 additional weeks.

TRY INSTEAD

The fermented tofu is ready to eat once it is transferred to the parchment-lined container. But if you let it cure for additional time, up to 8 weeks, its flavors will mellow and age. When young, it is quite salty, but over time, if you allow it to keep aging, it will turn into a lovely, cheeselike spread you can pair with crackers, bread, or vegetables.

NATTO

MAKES: 8 CUPS **PREP TIME:** 20 MINUTES, OVERNIGHT SOAKING, 3 TO 4 HOURS COOKING
FERMENTATION TIME: 24 HOURS

INTERMEDIATE

Natto is a food that people either love or hate—there is really no middle ground with this funky, sticky, gooey ferment. A Japanese staple, natto is commonly eaten for breakfast, dressed up with mustard, mayonnaise, or wasabi, and accompanied by rice and seaweed. This is a particularly smelly ferment, so it's a good idea to keep it somewhere isolated and apart from other foods that may absorb its odor or flavor. This recipe uses natto-moto, a specialized starter spore. When making natto, pay extra attention to sterilization to encourage the spores to do their work while not allowing other bacteria to grow. Boil all utensils that come into contact with natto for 5 minutes before using. Use a new cheesecloth, clean all surfaces, and wash your hands well before beginning.

2 pounds soybeans

1 spoonful natto-moto starter spores (use measuring spoon included with spores)

2 teaspoons sterile water

1. Cover the soybeans in about double their depth of water and soak overnight, or for about 12 hours.

2. The following day, drain the beans and place them in a large pot of fresh water. Bring the water to a boil and simmer for 3 to 4 hours, or until tender.

3. Drain the cooked beans and transfer them to a sterilized pot. Dissolve the natto spores in the sterilized water, and promptly add them to the warm beans. Stir the mixture together.

4. Distribute the beans among 3 or 4 large oven-safe containers, spreading a thin layer in each.

5. Cover each container with a piece of cheesecloth followed by a tight-fitting lid.

6. Place in either an oven with the pilot light set or in a dehydrator set to 100°F, and leave the beans for 24 hours.

7. Remove the beans from the oven or dehydrator, and let them cool for a couple of hours. Remove the cheesecloth from each container, replace the lid, and refrigerate the natto for at least 1 day before eating.

8. Refrigerated, natto keeps for 3 or 4 days. If not eaten within that period, natto can be frozen in individual serving sizes and then thawed prior to serving.

LEGUMES

7

SOY SAUCE

MAKES: 1 QUART **PREP TIME**:10 MINUTES, 24 HOURS SOAKING, 1 HOUR COOKING
FERMENTATION TIME: 2 MONTHS TO 1 YEAR

ADVANCED

Soy sauce, the ubiquitous liquid used in a variety of Asian dishes, can be made at home with a little skill and a whole lot of patience. Although you will have to wait about 6 months to taste your home-made creation, it will be well worth it when you are able to bottle your first batch. The process is an intense one with many steps, but you can cut down on labor by making a big batch annually. Skim off some of the younger soy sauce early to enjoy its lighter, mellow flavors in your cooking, and hold out for a year to get a product most like the typically dark sauce found in supermarkets.

2 cups whole soybeans
2 cups oat bran, toasted
2 cups water, plus more for soaking
3 tablespoons sea salt
½ cup barley koji

1. Cover the soybeans and toasted oat bran with water in a nonreactive bowl. Cover the bowl with a clean kitchen towel, and set aside to soak for 24 hours.

2. Drain the water and transfer the mixture to a steaming basket set over a pot. Fill the bottom of the pot with water and bring to a boil. Steam until the beans are tender, about 1 hour, and then cool completely.

3. Mix the beans and oat bran with the sea salt, and transfer the mixture to a food processor or blender. Process until the mixture is slightly chunky.

4. Add the barley koji to the mixture and stir well. Pack the paste into a half-gallon jar. Add the 2 cups water to the jar, leaving about 1 inch headspace at the top of the jar. Press the bean mixture down so that it is below the water level.

5. Affix a top on the jar loosely, so that gas is able to escape as it builds up during fermentation. If you have an air lock, use it here.

6. Keep the jar at room temperature and in a spot that is quite dark. Ferment the soy sauce for 2 months to 1 year, based on how you want the finished product to taste. Shorter fermentation time will yield a light, mild sauce, while longer fermentation time yields a dark, strong one.

7. Strain and bottle the soy sauce, and store in a cool pantry or similar area for up to 4 months.

A CLOSER LOOK

Soy sauce is a natural flavor enhancer and a great source of amino acids and glutamic acid, which aide the body in the digestive process. For the most benefit and best aroma, soy sauce should not be boiled, as much of its flavor is lost when cooked at high temperatures or for long periods. Instead, add soy sauce to foods during the last few minutes of cooking to season. Soy sauce makes a tasty addition to your table in place of salt, and can be used on both Western and Asian meats and vegetables, and in dressings and marinades to add flavor.

7

LEGUMES

8

MEAT & FISH

Many popular preserved meats use fermentation in their production process. More commonly called cured meats, foods such as prosciutto, pancetta, salami, and bacon undergo various degrees of fermentation during the curing process.

The technique of curing is loosely defined as various food preservation and flavoring processes used for meat, fish, and vegetable production that involve salt, sugar, nitrates, and nitrites. Some types of curing also entail smoking, as is the case with bacon, and even cooking. During the curing phase, sugar helps spur the growth of lactobacilli by providing food, creating a form of fermentation that is slowed considerably by the cool temperatures necessary for these types of fermentations to be safe.

Curing meat and fish changes their flavor and extends their shelf life. The most notable difference between meat and fish fermentations and the types previously covered in this book, such as fruit and vegetable fermentations, is that most take place under refrigeration. This necessary step ensures that these foods remain edible and that bad bacteria do not take hold, which can lead to spoilage and food-borne illness.

These projects require great attention to detail. There is little room for substitution when making meat and fish ferments, as the amounts and products used help protect the food from spoilage, not just provide seasoning. Planning is especially important to guarantee that these food items are produced in the manner indicated in these recipes.

Before beginning, review the "Cleaning and Safety" section of chapter 2 (page 28). Of particular importance in working with meat or fish is staying focused on the project you are working on to prevent cross-contamination in your kitchen.

This chapter is a primer on fermenting meat and fish. Most of the endeavors are relatively easy to undertake, and none requires expensive tools or equipment. If you become more interested in this area and wish to progress to advanced projects, such as fermented sausages, you will need to invest in a hygrometer to measure humidity in your aging room. But in this chapter, an instant-read kitchen thermometer is the only tool that is needed and that is only for Bacon (page 135).

For the Bacon recipe, you will also need equipment—a cold smoker to smoke the meat at a low enough temperature to kill bacteria while still maintaining the texture of the meat. This can be accomplished using a smoking basket and a variety of wood chips on a regular charcoal grill equipped with the aforementioned thermometer.

Pay special attention to the amounts and types of salt called for in meat and fish projects. For example, the Bacon recipe calls for pink sea salt, and the Pancetta recipe (page 136) calls for either pink sea salt or a mixture of sea salt and curing salt to protect the meat during curing. Other canning, pickling, or kosher salts cannot be used.

CORNED BEEF

MAKES: 3 POUNDS CORNED BEEF **PREP TIME:** 15 MINUTES, 3 HOURS COOKING
FERMENTATION TIME: 1 WEEK

BEGINNER

The easy route is pretty much always to choose the store-bought version of prepared corned beef. However, in true do-it-yourself spirit, this traditional corned beef can be made at home without all the nasty chemicals and preservatives used in a commercially processed corned beef. And you may be surprised just how easy the entire process really is. Requiring no special equipment, this is the perfect no-fuss project to get you started on meat fermentation and curing.

6 cups water

¾ cup sea salt

6 cloves garlic, crushed

4 bay leaves

1 stick cinnamon

2 tablespoons coriander seeds

2 tablespoons peppercorns

4 cloves

3 pounds beef brisket

1. Mix the water and salt in a small pan, and bring to a boil. Set aside to cool.

2. Mix the garlic and spices together in a small bowl, and place in a zippered plastic bag or large jar with a wide mouth. Place the brisket in the bag or jar.

3. Once cooled, add the brine to the bag or jar. If using a jar, weight the brisket down so that it stays submerged. Refrigerate the brisket for 1 week, flipping it after 3 days.

4. Remove the corned beef from the brine and dispose of the brine. In a large pot, soak the corned beef in cool water for 15 minutes to reduce the salt content. Discard the soaking water.

5. To cook, cover the corned beef with water, and simmer for 3 hours until tender.

6. To serve, slice thin strips from the corned beef. Refrigerate leftover corned beef for up to 1 week.

TRY INSTEAD

One of the wonderful things about corned beef is that once fermented, it can easily become a one-pot meal. Add potatoes, carrots, parsnips, cabbage, onions, rutabagas, or some combination of these vegetables to the cooking water to create a simple but scrumptious meal. Use the leftovers to throw together a hash of diced corned beef and potatoes for a filling breakfast, lunch, or dinner.

8

MEAT & FISH

MACKEREL

MAKES: 1 POUND   **PREP TIME:** 5 MINUTES, OVERNIGHT REST, 10 MINUTES
FERMENTATION TIME: 24 HOURS, 1 TO 2 WEEKS AGING

BEGINNER

Fermented mackerel is a delightful dish when served either raw or pan-fried. Using a blend of spices and herbs, this simple seafood dish is suddenly teeming with the flavors of fennel and pepper in just a few short days. Refrigerate it longer to further age it and develop more complex flavors. Select high-quality mackerel or substitute whole sardines or anchovies for a different (but still delightful) dish.

1 pound filleted mackerel
5 teaspoons sea salt, divided
1 cup water
2 tablespoons whey (page 23)
1 onion, sliced
1 fennel bulb, diced
1 teaspoon black pepper
¼ teaspoon red pepper flakes

1. Rinse the mackerel fillets in clean water and pat dry. Sprinkle the fillets on both sides with 1½ teaspoons of the salt and place them on a plate, covered with cheesecloth. Refrigerate overnight.

2. The following day, remove the cheesecloth and drain any liquid from the fish. Pat the fish dry using a paper towel or clean kitchen towel, and place it in a clean jar.

3. Prepare the brine by combining the water, remaining 3½ teaspoons salt, and all the other ingredients. Pour the brine over the fish.

4. Weight down the fish to keep it submerged in the brine, cover the jar with cheesecloth, and leave at room temperature for 24 hours.

5. The following day, place the lid on the jar and refrigerate the fish. The fillets will improve in flavor after about 1 or 2 weeks, and should be eaten within 1 month.

PAIR IT

Mix 1 cup fermented mackerel with ½ cup Crème Fraîche (page 85), a squeeze of lemon juice, and a dash each of salt and pepper to create a quick and easy fish spread. Try it on crackers or in a sandwich for a refreshing, filling treat.

SALMON

MAKES: 1 POUND **PREP TIME**: 15 MINUTES **FERMENTATION TIME**: 24 HOURS

BEGINNER

Salmon and dill are a classic pairing that gets a pickled twist in this recipe. Serve this salmon raw along with pickled shallots as part of a main course or appetizer for a simple but tangy and unexpected treat. Curing salmon extends its shelf life, allowing you to store this one-of-a-kind delicacy in the refrigerator for several weeks, during which time it will mellow and increase in complexity.

1 pound salmon, skinned

1 cup water

1 tablespoon sea salt

2 tablespoons whey (page 23)

1 tablespoon honey

1 cup shallots, peeled

1 teaspoon ground black pepper

1 bunch fresh dill fronds or 3 or 4 fresh dill heads

1 lemon, preferably organic

1. Cut the salmon into 1-inch chunks, and place in a clean 1-quart jar.

2. In a small bowl, mix all the remaining ingredients, except the lemon, stirring to dissolve the salt and honey. Slice the lemon thinly and add to the brine. Pour the brine over the salmon—the fish should be completely covered. If not, add more water until it is fully submerged. Place the lid on the jar, and leave the salmon at room temperature for 24 hours.

3. Move the salmon to the refrigerator. Serve with the pickled shallots and lemon slices.

MEAT & FISH

8

SHRIMP PASTE

MAKES: 1 CUP PREP TIME: 10 MINUTES, 20 MINUTES SOAK TIME
FERMENTATION TIME: 3 DAYS, 3 DAYS REFRIGERATION

BEGINNER

A classic seasoning for everything from soups to curries to sauces in Southeast Asian cooking, homemade shrimp paste is a vibrantly bright condiment with a pungent aroma and big flavor, unlike store-bought versions, which tend to fall flat in both color and complexity. If you are having trouble finding whole dried shrimp, check out a local Asian or Latino market, where they are generally available.

1 ounce dried whole shrimp

4 or 5 dried Thai chiles

1 garlic clove

½ teaspoon sugar

1 teaspoon sea salt

1 teaspoon Fish Sauce (page 134)

1 tablespoon whey (page 23)

1. Place the shrimp in a small pan and cover with water. Bring to a boil, cook for about 3 minutes, turn off the heat, and leave them to steep for 20 minutes.

2. Drain the shrimp, reserving the cooking water.

3. Place the chiles in a bowl, and cover them with the hot cooking water. Set aside to rehydrate for about 20 minutes.

4. Add the shrimp, rehydrated chiles, garlic, sugar, salt, and fish sauce to a blender, and process for just a few seconds, until chunky. Add the whey and a bit of the cooking water—add about a tablespoon at a time—until you have a smooth paste. Purée until very smooth.

5. Transfer to a jar, cover it, and leave the shrimp paste to ferment at room temperature for 3 days. Refrigerate it for 3 more days before using. Open and use within 2 months.

GRAVLAX

MAKES: 1 POUND **PREP TIME**: 15 MINUTES **FERMENTATION TIME**: 2 TO 6 DAYS

INTERMEDIATE

Gravlax is quite an expensive treat when purchased from a local deli, but you can easily make it at home with great results and at a fraction of the cost. In as little as two days, you can turn an ordinary piece of salmon into this special dish with just a few supplies. Remove the pin bones from the salmon before beginning by using pliers, and then get started on this New York classic.

1 pound salmon fillet, cut from the midsection of the fish

2 tablespoons sea salt

1 tablespoon green peppercorns, crushed

2 tablespoons honey

2 tablespoons whey (page 23)

1 bunch fresh dill

1. Rinse the salmon and pat it dry. Cut it into 2 equal pieces.

2. Place the salmon pieces on a large piece of plastic wrap, flesh side up.

3. Mix the salt, green peppercorns, and honey together, and then rub the mixture into the flesh of the salmon.

4. Drizzle the whey over both pieces, and rub it in as well. Arrange the dill onto one piece of the salmon.

5. Flip the piece of salmon without the dill on top of the other, so that the flesh sides are touching. Wrap them together tightly in the plastic wrap, and place them on a plate. Put another plate on top of the fish, and add a heavy object on top of it, such as a rock, to apply weight. Refrigerate the fish like this for 2 to 6 days, flipping the plates with the fish every 12 hours to redistribute the juices.

6. When it is time to serve the gravlax, unwrap it, and slice it very thinly on the diagonal.

FISH SAUCE

MAKES: 2 CUPS PREP TIME: 20 MINUTES, 3 DAYS RESTING
FERMENTATION TIME: 6 TO 10 WEEKS

INTERMEDIATE

Making fish sauce is a labor of love. Not because it is difficult but because it is a stinky process that is not for the faint of heart. An essential ingredient of many South Asian cuisines, most notably Thai and Vietnamese, this smelly process creates a sauce that is, surprisingly, not too stinky at all. If you use fish sauce regularly, consider doubling or tripling the batch so that you can make it a biannual tradition instead of a bimonthly chore.

1½ pounds mackerel, sardines, anchovies, or a combination

3 garlic cloves

5 tablespoons sea salt, divided

2 cups water

1 teaspoon peppercorns, crushed

2 to 3 strips lemon peel

2 tablespoons fermented pickling brine or whey (page 23)

1. Cut the fish into 1-inch chunks. In a food processor or using a mortar and pestle, process the fish until it forms a slurry. Place the fish in a jar.

2. Smash the garlic cloves and add to the jar. Add 3 tablespoons of the sea salt and all the remaining ingredients to the jar. Mix thoroughly. If the fish is not covered, add more water until it is fully submerged. Cover the jar and leave it at room temperature to rest for 3 days.

3. Stir in the remaining 2 tablespoons sea salt, and leave the fish sauce to ferment for 6 weeks, opening the jar every couple of days to release gas. Alternatively, use a jar with an air lock to avoid this regular maintenance.

4. Taste the fish sauce at 6 weeks. If you like the flavor, it is done. If not, leave it for up to 4 more weeks to ferment.

5. When the taste is to your liking, strain the fish sauce through a wire mesh strainer into a bottle, seal it, label it, and refrigerate. Fish sauce keeps in the refrigerator for 6 months.

BACON

MAKES: 2½ POUNDS BACON **PREP TIME:** 10 MINUTES, 3 HOURS SMOKING
FERMENTATION TIME: 5 TO 7 DAYS

ADVANCED

Bacon is one of the most loved and most widely eaten cured meats. Known by some aficionados as "pig candy" or "meat candy," bacon is made when pork belly is transformed using sugar, salt, and spice. Finished by cold smoking, which imparts a whole host of additional flavors, this project is well worth the work. There is really no comparison between a homemade slab of bacon and store-bought bacon, and if you try this recipe, you'll taste that home-cured is the winner with just one bite.

6 cups water

2 cups pink sea salt

1 cup maple or palm sugar

1 tablespoon crushed peppercorns

2½ pounds pork belly, skin removed

1. In a large bowl, combine the water, pink sea salt, sugar, and peppercorns, and stir until the sugar and salt are dissolved. Place the pork belly into this brine, and weight it down with a plate so that the entire surface of the pork is submerged. Cover the bowl with a clean kitchen towel, and place it in the refrigerator.

2. Check on the pork belly daily to be certain that it remains fully submerged. Leave it in the brine for 5 to 7 days. When the pork belly begins to feel solid, like an inflated ball, it is ready to be smoked.

3. Remove the bacon from the brine and rinse it off. Prepare a cold smoker to 200°F. Place a variety of wood chips as desired directly on the coals. For bacon, using a mixture of wood chips, including apple, hickory, and mesquite, imparts a good flavor.

4. Smoke the bacon for 3 hours. The internal temperature of the meat should reach 150°F to kill any bacteria and give the bacon a good smoky flavor, while still leaving it in a state that can be cooked later. Use an instant-read thermometer to ensure that the internal temperature of the bacon is 150°F before removing it from the smoker.

5. Cut the bacon into thin strips. Keep in an airtight container in the refrigerator for 3 to 5 days, or freeze to extend the storage time.

8

MEAT & FISH

PANCETTA

MAKES: 2 POUNDS **PREP TIME**: 15 MINUTES
FERMENTATION TIME: 1 WEEK, 1 WEEK DRYING TIME

ADVANCED

Pancetta is a cured meat that is commonly known as Italian bacon. Flavored with herbs and spices, it is a savory alternative to smoked and sometimes sweetened breakfast meat. Making pancetta requires pink sea salt, which has naturally occurring nitrates to help preserve the meat. If pink sea salt is unavailable, use a mixture of 3 tablespoons sea salt and 1 tablespoon curing salt instead. Other supplies for this recipe include kitchen twine and a cool, dark room in which to finish the meat.

1 teaspoon dried thyme
1 teaspoon dried rosemary
½ teaspoon paprika
2 teaspoons peppercorns, crushed
2½ pounds pork belly, skin removed
¼ cup pink sea salt

1. Create an herb-and-spice rub by mixing the thyme, rosemary, paprika, and peppercorns together in a small bowl. Coat the pork belly with this mixture.

2. Rub the pink sea salt on to all sides of the pork, and then press any remaining herb-and-spice mixture into the meat.

3. Place the pork belly into a plastic zippered bag, pushing out as much air as possible before sealing the bag. Place the bag in the refrigerator for several days. When the belly begins to lose some moisture, begin checking it for readiness—wait for the meat to become firmed, similar to the feel of a flexed muscle. This process should take about 1 week.

4. Remove the belly from the bag, and brush off the herbs, spices, and meat from the surface of the belly. Because the herbs and spices have a tendency to grow mold, be sure to meticulously remove all of them before moving on to the next step.

5. Lay the belly flat on a clean work surface with the skin side down. Roll it into a cylindrical shape toward your body, as tightly as you can. Tie the belly with a few pieces of kitchen string so that it holds its shape. Leave a piece of the twine longer to enable you to hang the meat.

6. Hang the pork in a cool, dark place for 1 week. A basement or cellar is typically the best place. Make a note on the calendar or set a reminder so that you don't forget to check it after 1 week.

7. At 1 week, the pancetta will have browned slightly, it will be firm, and once the strings are snipped, it will not readily unroll.

8. Refrigerate the pancetta until ready to use; it can be stored for several weeks. When ready to eat, slice a few strips or cubes from the belly, and fry as you would bacon.

TRY INSTEAD

Because pancetta is cured in a large amount of salt, the flavor may be too salty for you. If so, boil the pancetta for 1 minute before cooking to remove some of the salt. Discard the water, drain the pancetta, and proceed as usual with your recipe.

9

VINEGARS & CONDIMENTS

Vinegars and condiments are often overlooked, but their role in preparing, flavoring, and presenting our foods is a considerable one. Beginning with quality fresh ingredients will yield bright, flavorful vinegars and condiments that have countless uses in the kitchen and on the table.

The recipes in this chapter will provide you with a solid base of fermentable condiments and probiotic additions to your meals. Whether you are interested in using vinegars to create quick pickles, salads, or sauces, there is enough variety here that you can forgo store-bought vinegars (which are often made using genetically modified ingredients) once you amass a collection of bottles for your homemade concoctions.

Condiments such as ketchup, mustard, and barbecue sauce are an easy way to boost the amount of healthy bacteria you are eating daily, thus improving digestion and overall health. Kids, who may otherwise balk at the idea of eating fermented foods, are happy to consume these flavorful sauces. The fermented chutneys here can easily double as dipping sauces for a number of breads and meats, making them indispensable at your table.

All the recipes in this chapter are beginner recipes. There are no extra tools or accessories required for these either, making them easy to get started with right away.

The one product that you will absolutely need for many of these recipes, aside from whey (page 23), is raw, unfiltered apple cider vinegar.

This type of apple cider vinegar contains the "mother," a gelatinous blob composed of acetic acid bacteria that is responsible for converting the cider into vinegar. This type of apple cider vinegar is teeming with beneficial bacteria to get a ferment going. Pasteurized apple cider vinegar, the type most commonly found in supermarkets, is no substitute for raw, unfiltered apple cider vinegar. Once pasteurized, the living bacteria are killed and so cannot be used for future culturing.

One last word of advice: Do not use any homemade vinegars for canning purposes without testing their strength using a pH meter first. Vinegar used for canning is typically around 5 percent acetic acid, which works to protect canned items from spoilage in an anaerobic environment. Acidified canned foods that use a water bath method (pickles, sauerkraut, salsa) must have a pH lower than 4.6 to prevent the growth of *Clostridium botulinum* spores, making the pH of the vinegar of prime importance.

APPLE CIDER VINEGAR

MAKES: 1 QUART **PREP TIME:** 10 MINUTES **FERMENTATION TIME:** 4 TO 5 WEEKS

BEGINNER

Making your own raw apple cider vinegar saves you big-time, especially if you use this multipurpose workhorse regularly in the kitchen. Use it to dress a salad, flavor a pickle, add to your bone broth, or prepare any number of other favorite dishes. Use a mix of sweet and tart apples to create a more complex vinegar. Or purchase a jug of unpasteurized apple cider with no additives from the store, and get started on your very own batch of this liquid gold.

2 apples or scraps from 4 apples
3¾ cups water
¼ cup honey

1. Add the apples to a large jar. Mix the water and honey together, and pour over the apples. Cover the jar with a clean kitchen towel, and leave in a warm location. Gently shake the jar once a day to mix up the contents.

2. After about a week, the pieces of apple will begin to sink to the bottom as alcohol fermentation ends. When this occurs, strain the now hard cider away from the apples, and return the cider to a clean jar. Cover with a clean kitchen towel secured with a rubber band. Leave in a warm location.

3. After 3 to 4 weeks, the vinegar should be finished. Test it at 3 weeks and if ready, bottle it into an airtight swing-top bottle. If not, leave it an additional week, or until it has that signature, vinegary tang, and then bottle.

PAIR IT

Use your homemade apple cider vinegar to make a master cleansing tonic to prevent illness during flu season. Chop equal amounts of ginger, chiles, onions, horseradish root, and garlic. Place them in a jar. Cover completely with apple cider vinegar, screw on the lid, and leave in a cool, dark location for 1 week. Strain the apple cider vinegar away from the solids, and store in a sealed container. Drink a small amount of this tonic daily, or use it to season fresh foods.

VINEGARS & CONDIMENTS

9

HONEY VINEGAR

MAKES: 1 QUART **PREP TIME**: 15 MINUTES **FERMENTATION TIME**: 8 WEEKS

BEGINNER

Honey vinegar is as unique and floral as the honey from which it came. Always use raw honey for this ferment, and experiment with different types of honey, as there are many different types and flavors of this natural sweet treat. Clover and wildflower varieties are typically quite mild, while other kinds, such as carrot honey, have peppery and spicy undertones that would make an intriguingly complex honey vinegar.

1 cup honey
2 cups warm water

1. Mix honey and water together in a jar. Cover the jar with a clean kitchen towel secured with a rubber band. Place in a warm, dark location for 8 weeks.

2. After 8 weeks, the honey should have transformed into alcohol and then vinegar, and fermentation will have stopped; you will know because it will be clear in color. Bottle the finished vinegar in an airtight swing-top bottle, and store until ready to use.

RED WINE VINEGAR

MAKES: 2 CUPS **PREP TIME:** 5 MINUTES **FERMENTATION TIME:** 4 TO 6 WEEKS

BEGINNER

Red wine vinegar lends a complex, warming flavor to foods. Requiring just two ingredients, this is about as simple as it gets. Factor in a bit of patience, and you have a condiment that can easily become the basis for a wonderful salad dressing or marinade.

2 cups red wine, plus more for topping off
6 tablespoons apple cider vinegar

1. Mix the red wine and vinegar together in a jar. Cover with a clean kitchen towel secured with a rubber band. Place in a warm location, and leave to ferment for 4 weeks.

2. Occasionally throughout the fermentation process, use the extra red wine to top off the vinegar as it evaporates.

3. After 4 weeks, taste the vinegar. If it tastes sour and tangy, transfer it to an airtight container, such as a swing-top bottle. If not, leave it to ferment for an additional 2 weeks, and then bottle the vinegar.

FRUIT VINEGAR

MAKES: 1 QUART **PREP TIME:** 5 MINUTES **FERMENTATION TIME:** 6 WEEKS

BEGINNER

9

Customize this recipe with your favorite fruit to make a vinegar fit for a one-of-a-kind salad dressing, marinade, or sauce. This works well with plums, pears, raspberries, blackberries, or even tomatoes to make a sweet, flavorful vinegar that complements seasonal summer dishes spectacularly. To save money and prevent waste, use bruised or smashed fruits (or even fruit peels and cores) when making this, as it makes no difference in the finished product.

2 cups chopped fruit, fruit peels, fruit cores, or a combination

¼ cup honey

4 cups water

1. Pack the fruit pieces or scraps into a large jar.

2. Mix the water and honey until dissolved. Use room temperature water, rather than cold, or heat the water until lukewarm to help the honey dissolve. Pour the honey-water over the fruit pieces. Cover the container with a clean kitchen towel secured with a rubber band, and place the jar in a warm location to ferment for 6 weeks.

3. Set up a wire mesh strainer over a funnel, and then pour the vinegar through it into a clean bottle. Cap, label, and store until use.

WHOLE-GRAIN MUSTARD

MAKES: 2 CUPS **PREP TIME:** 10 MINUTES **FERMENTATION TIME:** 3 TO 5 DAYS

BEGINNER

Mustard is easy to grab off the shelf and so inexpensive that seeking an alternative may just seem unnecessary. But you can make it at home in just a few minutes longer than it would take to grab your favorite jar at the store. This simple but boldly flavored condiment is so easy to get right that you may wonder why you ever bought it premade. With a mix of yellow and brown mustard seeds, this whole-grain, country-style mustard has plenty of bite for all kinds of sandwiches and other dishes, but it is not overwhelming, making it a perfect all-purpose mustard to substitute for the standard yellow.

½ cup whole yellow mustard seeds, divided
½ cup whole brown mustard seeds, divided
¾ cup water
2 tablespoons honey
¼ cup whey (page 23)
2 teaspoons sea salt
Juice of 1 lemon

1. Using a mortar and pestle, lightly crush half the mustard seeds (¼ cup yellow and ¼ cup brown). If you don't have a mortar and pestle, place the seeds in a zippered plastic storage bag and gently split them using a mallet or other kitchen tool.

2. Add the crushed seeds, remaining whole seeds, and the rest of the ingredients to a jar. Mix well, cover with a lid, and store at room temperature for 3 to 5 days. Then transfer to the refrigerator, where the mustard will keep for several months.

TRY INSTEAD

To make this mustard creamy, once it is complete, transfer the mustard to a blender or use an immersion blender to process it. Don't substitute ground powder for whole mustard seeds to expedite the process—the seeds pack a lot more flavor than the powder does, which typically loses its flavor much quicker due to oxidation.

KETCHUP

MAKES: 2 CUPS **PREP TIME:** 10 MINUTES **FERMENTATION TIME:** 3 TO 5 DAYS

BEGINNER

At one time ketchup was a condiment devoid of high amounts of sugar, but in today's world, every brand available is super sweet, boasting high fructose corn syrup and other highly processed sweeteners. Avoid added sugar and get some serious probiotic benefit into everyday foods by making this easy fermented ketchup at home.

1½ cups tomato paste

¼ cup honey

⅓ cup water

¼ cup whey (page 23)

2 tablespoons apple cider vinegar

½ teaspoon ground allspice

⅛ teaspoon ground cinnamon

⅛ teaspoon ground cloves

⅛ teaspoon freshly ground black pepper

1 teaspoon sea salt

1. Mix the tomato paste, honey, water, whey, and vinegar in a jar. Sprinkle the spices and salt into the jar, and stir gently to combine.

2. Cover the jar with a lid, and place the jar in a warm location for 3 to 5 days, or until the contents are noticeably bubbly. Refrigerate and begin using immediately or store for several months.

BARBECUE SAUCE

MAKES: ABOUT 2 CUPS **PREP TIME:** 10 MINUTES **FERMENTATION TIME:** 2 DAYS

BEGINNER

Check out the label on a store-bought bottle of barbecue sauce, and you likely will see many preservatives and a whole lot of sugar. Avoid the unnecessary additives, extend the shelf life of your barbecue sauce naturally, and skip all the added sugar when you make this ribs-worthy sauce at home. This recipe makes about a pint, but can easily be scaled up to make more for a large gathering. To retain its probiotic benefit, slather this barbecue sauce on foods at the end of cooking.

1¼ cups tomato paste

6 tablespoons honey

2 tablespoons apple cider vinegar

2 tablespoons soy sauce

1 teaspoon dry mustard powder

⅛ tablespoon garlic powder

½ teaspoon chili powder

¼ teaspoon cayenne

½ teaspoon salt

1 tablespoon whey (page 23)

1. Mix all the ingredients except the whey in a wide-mouth pint jar. Once everything is combined, add the whey on top and gently stir it into the sauce.

2. Cover the jar with a lid, and place the jar in a warm location for 2 days. Then refrigerate the barbecue sauce until ready to use.

VINEGARS & CONDIMENTS

9

MINT CHUTNEY

MAKES: 1 CUP **PREP TIME**: 10 MINUTES **FERMENTATION TIME**: 2 DAYS

BEGINNER

Mint chutney pairs as well with Western-style grilled chicken as it does with Indian grilled meats. This bright and complex chutney is perfect to make during the spring and summer, when mint is in abundance. If you have some extra space in your yard or on a patio, add a potted mint plant and reap the benefits of the harvest of this prolific grower.

2 cups loosely packed mint leaves

1 cup loosely packed cilantro

1 small onion, peeled and chopped

2 garlic cloves, peeled

2 jalapeños, cored and seeded

1 teaspoon ground cumin

1½-inch piece of ginger, chopped

2 teaspoons sea salt

4 tablespoons plain whole milk yogurt

1. Add all the ingredients except the salt and yogurt to a blender, and process until they are a smooth paste.

2. Transfer the mixture to a jar, and stir in the salt and yogurt. Cover with a clean kitchen towel, and leave to ferment in a warm location for 2 days. Refrigerate before serving.

VINEGARS & CONDIMENTS

9

COCONUT CHUTNEY

MAKES: 2 CUPS **PREP TIME:** 15 MINUTES **FERMENTATION TIME:** 2 TO 4 DAYS

BEGINNER

Coconut chutney is one of the traditional sauces used for dipping Dosa (page 116). A sweet and sour sauce, it's simple to make, and when fermented, it adds just the right amount of tang to balance the dosa's crisp texture and soured flavor. If you reconstitute dried and shredded coconut, this recipe is easily accessible year-round and takes very little time to throw together. Serve it cold.

1 cup shredded, unsweetened coconut

2 tablespoons canola oil

3 tablespoons coarsely ground chickpeas

Juice of 1 lemon

1 teaspoon salt

1 teaspoon cumin seeds

1 teaspoon coriander seeds

1 tablespoon honey

1½-inch ginger knob, sliced

1 small chile

½ teaspoon mustard seeds

½ teaspoon asafetida

¾ cup Kefir (page 79)

1. Soak the coconut in ½ cup warm water until reconstituted.

2. Heat oil in a small frying pan. Add the chickpeas and fry for a few seconds, until they begin to darken.

3. Combine the fried chickpeas, lemon juice, salt, cumin, coriander, honey, ginger, chile, and reconstituted coconut in a blender and process until smooth.

4. Add the mustard seeds to the frying pan, and fry until they start to pop. Add the asafetida and half of the kefir, mixing well.

5. Mix the rest of the kefir, the mustard seed–kefir mixture, and the coconut mixture together in a jar. Cover with a clean kitchen towel, and leave to ferment in a warm location for 2 to 4 days. Refrigerate to cool before using.

VINEGARS & CONDIMENTS

9

FERMENTED GARLIC

MAKES: 1 PINT **PREP TIME:** 5 MINUTES **FERMENTATION TIME:** 7 DAYS, 7 DAYS REFRIGERATED

BEGINNER

Fermented garlic can be used in both raw and cooked dishes to provide a slightly tangier yet mellower flavor. Try it as the dressing base in our Ultimate Salad (page 181), or use it any way you like to use ordinary garlic. If peeling enough garlic to make a decent-size batch sounds like a chore you don't want to undertake, look for peeled and packaged fresh garlic in the refrigerated section of your grocery store to make prep a breeze.

1½ tablespoons sea salt
1 cup water
1¾ cups garlic cloves, peeled

1. Make a brine using 1½ tablespoons of salt per 1 cup of water.

2. Place the garlic cloves in a jar. Pour the brine over the cloves to cover them. Use a weight to hold them below the surface.

3. Affix the lid to the jar, or use a lid fitted with an air lock. Keep the jar at room temperature for 7 days. After 7 days, move the jar to the refrigerator for another 7 days before using.

PAIR IT

In many cultures, garlic is used as a remedy to prevent and treat cold and flu. Steep this fermented garlic in honey (completely covered) for 2 to 3 days and then eat it. The subsequent garlic-flavored honey can be taken on its own or mixed into a glass of hot water to help treat a cold or flu.

RANCH DRESSING

MAKES 1 PINT **PREP TIME:** 10 MINUTES **FERMENTATION TIME:** 1 DAY

BEGINNER

Store-bought salad dressings are filled with preservatives, sugar, and often a long list of unpronounceable ingredients. Skip the added fillers, and make this simple ranch dressing that you will feel good about eating. Sour cream gives the dressing a thickened, creamy texture, while the herbs season it just right so that it tastes like a traditional ranch dressing.

1½ cups Kefir (page 79)

¼ cup sour cream

4 medium garlic cloves, minced

½ teaspoon black pepper

2 tablespoons parsley

1 teaspoon salt

1½ tablespoons fresh lemon juice

1½ teaspoons dried onion powder

Place all the ingredients in a jar and mix well. Cover the jar and leave to ferment at room temperature for 1 day. Transfer to the refrigerator.

PREPARATION TIP

This dressing can easily be turned into a dip by separating the kefir from its whey, resulting in a thicker, creamier ranch dip. Do this by pouring the dressing into a wire mesh strainer lined with a cheesecloth or a few coffee filters and set over a bowl. Once the whey has dripped out, transfer the dip to an airtight container and refrigerate until ready for use. If you wish to reserve the whey for other uses, complete this step before adding the spices so that the whey is not flavored.

10

BREWS

Long before bottled and canned sodas were available at every market and store, the fermentation of beverages was a regular practice performed in the home. Even with the advent of multinational soda companies, in many parts of the world, home beverage making still regularly takes place. Many of these traditional beverage ferments have gained recognition and have been given new life in the DIY fermenting community of today.

In the West, this type of home brewing has gained significant momentum in the past few decades, as many people wish to create drinks without high levels of sugar or unpronounceable, unnatural ingredients. This artisan craft is experiencing its largest growth in generations.

Though extremely popular, beer and wine aren't the only fermented beverages you can make at home; a whole host of less potent brews can be made from a variety of ingredients. Not only are these nonalcoholic drinks intensely tasty, but they also have all of the same beneficial bacteria needed for healthy digestion. Instead of filling your gut with empty calories from sodas, you can fill it with what it needs to function properly.

There are other alcoholic fermented beverages you can make as well. From mead to wine to beer to hard cider, many beverage projects are readily accessible to the home brewer.

ALCOHOLIC FERMENTATION VESSELS

Once you get into making wine and beer, a few items make the job much easier and allow you to get more accurate results. The primary fermentation of alcohol, or the portion of the process that converts most of the sugars to alcohol, requires oxygen. In order for the yeast to be active and thrive, they need an adequate supply of oxygen. An open-top fermenter, such as a food-grade plastic bucket, large glass jar, or other food-safe item, will work just fine.

Once alcohol is created, however, acetic bacteria, as well as many other types of food-spoiling organisms, can turn your alcohol bad in a flash. Many of these bacteria—most notably acetobacter—need oxygen to survive, making it necessary to eliminate oxygen from the mix to protect your brew. At this point in the procedure, you will need a vessel that locks out air to finish your fermented beverage. A 1-gallon glass jug is suitable for the recipes in this chapter, while larger projects will most likely require a 5-gallon carboy. You will also need a bung, which looks like a giant rubber stopper with a hole drilled in its top, and an air lock to attach to it for all the recipes in this chapter.

ALCOHOLIC FERMENTATION TOOLS AND SUPPLIES

Although not necessary, a hydrometer is a handy tool for alcohol fermentation. Used to measure the amount of sugar in the beginning juice (aka must) in order to both gauge the final alcohol content, and determine when primary fermentation is complete, a hydrometer is an inexpensive addition to your kitchen. To use, the glass tool is submerged in a testing tube filled with the liquid that you will be fermenting. Depending on how high it floats in the liquid, you can determine how much sugar is in the liquid and its potential alcohol content.

Alcohol fermentation, especially with beer and wine, requires a higher level of sanitation than other fermenting projects. Because beer and wine sit for extended periods, you must wash and sanitize all utensils and items that come in contact with the beer or wine throughout the process to prevent spoilage or contamination. Any home brew shop can recommend a good cleaner and sanitizer.

A wine thief—a tool used to remove samples of wine or beer for testing—is handy but not necessary when you are starting out. Some plastic tubing and an auto-siphon are recommended to transfer wine, mead, beer, or hard cider without disturbing the sediment at the bottom of its vessel.

STORAGE OF FERMENTED BEVERAGES

Although still fermented beverages do not require special storage containers, carbonated fermented beverages, such as flavored kombucha, water kefirs, or beer, require containers made to withstand added pressure. Swing-top beer bottles are the best way to store these beverages, and they are available in various sizes from home brew shops. These bottles can be reused, making them a cost-effective and environmentally friendly solution. Grolsch beer, a commercially manufactured lager, is sold in this type of bottle. A good bottle brush makes cleaning these containers a breeze.

ALCOHOL FERMENTATION AND SANITATION

When making alcoholic ferments, sanitation is of top priority, as it is the difference between a drinkable product and one that is overpowered by off-flavors and odors. When home wine or beer making fails, the most likely reason is lack of proper sanitation.

Washing equipment in a commercial cleaner that does not foam is particularly valuable when you begin making larger batches or have a lot of bottles to clean—you will find the foaming action of household dishwashing liquid very frustrating to rinse entirely out of equipment. Once items are cleaned, they must also be sanitized. To avoid having to buy more products, use Campden tablets, which are called for in the Red Wine recipe (page 172) for sanitation. Crush four tablets and dissolve them in a quart of cool water. Rinse all equipment that comes in contact with the wine in this solution, and allow the equipment to air dry before using.

KOMBUCHA

MAKES: ABOUT 8 CUPS **PREP TIME:** 20 MINUTES **FERMENTATION TIME:** 7 TO 10 DAYS

BEGINNER

Produced through the fermentation of tea and sugar, kombucha is a health beverage that has seen a recent boom in popularity. Forget about paying exorbitant prices for a 10-ounce bottle when you can create well-balanced and flavorful kombucha at home. Start with this simple recipe for fermenting the stronger-flavored black tea. Once you understand the underlying process, you can experiment with different types of teas, such as oolong or green, to discover their unique flavors.

6¾ cups water, divided
½ cup sugar
4 black tea bags
1 SCOBY (page 14)
1 cup starter kombucha

1. In a small saucepan on the stovetop, bring 2 cups of the water just to a boil, or 212°F. Add the sugar and stir to dissolve (see fig. A). Place the tea bags in the water and steep, covered, for 10 minutes. Squeeze each tea bag against the side of the pot, using a stainless steel spoon to extract as much liquid as possible. Remove the tea bags from the pot, and compost or discard them.

2. In a half-gallon jar, add the remaining 4¾ cups water, along with the sweetened tea (see fig. B). Use a thermometer to ensure that the water is 72°F or cooler before proceeding. It is very important to test the temperature. Failure to do so can result in the death of the cultures in the SCOBY and the starter tea.

3. With clean hands, place the SCOBY on the surface of the sweetened tea, and add the starter kombucha (see fig. C). The SCOBY may float on the surface or sink farther down into the tea. There should be about 1 inch between the SCOBY and the top of the jar, so that it does not touch the cover that will go on the jar. If there is not enough room, draw out a little of the tea with a cup and throw it away.

4. Cover the jar with a clean kitchen towel secured with a rubber band (see fig. D).

5. Place the jar in a warm location that is away from direct sunlight, and where the ambient temperature ranges from 72°F to 78°F.

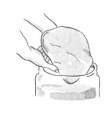

6. After 7 days, place a straw into the kombucha along the side of the jar, so as not to disturb the SCOBY, and cover the other end with your finger to capture some kombucha in the straw (see fig. E). Remove the straw and taste the kombucha. If it tastes good, you are done. If it is too sweet, continue fermentation for a few more days and then taste it again.

7. With clean, rinsed hands, remove the SCOBY and place it in a glass or porcelain bowl (see fig. F). Cover the SCOBY with about 1 cup of the finished kombucha. This will be your starter for your next batch. If you plan to use the SCOBY right away, leave it out until you are ready to use it. To make a batch later, place the SCOBY and the kombucha starter into a jar, cover the jar with a lid, and store the SCOBY and the kombucha starter in the refrigerator for up to 3 weeks between batches. When ready to use, leave the SCOBY and the kombucha starter on the counter until it comes to room temperature and start all over again.

8. When you've decided that it's time to store your kombucha, place a funnel over a swing-top bottle and pour the kombucha into it, leaving about an inch of headspace in the neck of the bottle (see fig. G). Tightly cap the bottle and refrigerate the kombucha to enjoy now, or leave it on the counter for another day or two to complete a secondary fermentation.

BREWS

10

KOMBUCHA TROUBLESHOOTING TIPS

- After one or two batches, you will notice that your SCOBY is expanding and getting thicker. This is normal, a sign that it is working well. But it will need to be separated to slow its fermentation of subsequent batches. To do this, using clean hands, separate the layers by gently pulling them apart into two thinner rounds. In some cases, they can be fused together pretty tightly, making this task difficult. If that is the case, simply cut the SCOBY in half.

- Once you separate your SCOBY, you can keep a backup in your refrigerator in case something goes wrong during the fermentation process. You can also give backups to friends interested in brewing kombucha. Always store a SCOBY in enough kombucha that it is completely covered.

- Kombucha is loaded with natural yeasts, which can present themselves as stringy, gloppy brown strands. Between batches, you can minimize these by carefully rinsing your SCOBY to remove any strands. To prevent these appearing in the finished product, strain the kombucha through a fine mesh strainer before bottling or serving.

- Kombucha can be made with black, green, or oolong tea. But mixing together the SCOBYs used for each can result in some strange off-flavors. If you are going to ferment different types of tea for kombucha, keep a SCOBY dedicated to each type to maintain a consistent flavor profile for the finished drinks.

BLUEBERRY-GINGER KOMBUCHA

MAKES: 1 QUART **PREP TIME:** 5 MINUTES **FERMENTATION TIME:** 2 DAYS

BEGINNER

Although kombucha can taste great on its own, it is even more invigorating when combined with fruits, spices, and herbs to create distinctive flavor combinations. Called secondary fermentation, this second stage of kombucha making also produces carbonation, making a fruity, bubbly kombucha, similar to a soda. A good amount of carbonation can be created in only 2 days of secondary fermentation, and the process should not be prolonged, as the sugars in the drink can be converted to alcohol, turning this all-ages treat into a non-family-friendly beverage.

½ cup blueberries
1 (1-inch) piece fresh ginger
4 cups kombucha

1. Put the blueberries into a quart jar. Cut the ginger into thin pieces, and add them to the jar.

2. Pour the kombucha into the jar as well, and cover tightly with a lid. Leave in a warm location for 2 days.

3. Open the jar daily to prevent gas buildup. After 2 days, refrigerate until cold and serve. If desired, strain the kombucha before drinking to remove any mother or fruit solids. If not enjoying the same day, pour the kombucha into swing-top bottles using a funnel, close the bottles, and refrigerate until ready to drink.

TRY INSTEAD

Use your imagination when flavoring kombucha—unexpected combinations can produce amazing results. Some simple ingredient pairings: orange and fennel, strawberry and vanilla, or ginger and just about any fruit. Stick with the same ratio of about ½ cup of fruit to each quart of kombucha. For extracts, use no more than 1 teaspoon per quart, and for both fresh and dried herbs, experiment with amounts.

BREWS

10

WATER KEFIR

Water kefir uses a type of "grains" similar to what milk kefir uses, but because a sugar-water combination is used to make it, water kefir is a great alternative if you don't consume or tolerate dairy. The bacteria used here eats up a lot of the sugar in the water, leaving you with many strains of good bacteria, along with a pleasant, lightly sweet taste. Water kefir has fewer bacteria strains than milk kefir yet more than other popular dairy ferments, such as yogurt. When you are done with the water kefir, consume it plain, or proceed to secondary fermentation to add some effervescence and additional flavors, such as fruits, herbs, and extracts.

3⅞ cups water, divided
¼ cup sugar
¼ cup water kefir grains

1. In a small pot, bring 1 cup of the water to a boil. Add the sugar to the pot and stir until dissolved. Turn off the heat.

2. Measure the remaining 2⅞ cups water into a quart jar. Once slightly cooled, add the sugar-water mixture in and stir.

3. When the water is lukewarm, add the kefir grains to the jar. Cover with a lid and place in a warm location for 2 to 4 days. Strain out the grains and serve, bottle the water kefir, or proceed to secondary fermentation. Refrigerate if not drinking immediately.

ALTERNATIVE PREPARATIONS USING WATER KEFIR GRAINS

If you aren't interested in brewing with sugar-water, consider using water kefir grains to make other beverages, such as fermented coconut water; soy, nut, and grain milks; or fruit and vegetable juices. To culture these beverages, measure out the same amount of liquid used in the basic recipe for water kefir, and ferment for 24 to 48 hours. Be careful not to overferment, as this can result in alcohol production. When making these alternative beverages, make a batch of water kefir in between other drinks to keep the grains healthy.

RASPBERRY LEMONADE WATER KEFIR

MAKES: 1 QUART **PREP TIME:** 5 MINUTES, 5 MINUTES FOLLOWING 2 DAYS
FERMENTATION TIME: 3 DAYS

BEGINNER

Skip the lemonade stand and try this probiotic blend instead. Like kombucha and milk kefir, water kefir can be dressed up to suit your personal taste. Fruit blends shine in water kefir, which has a residual sweetness, and the beverage pairs really wonderfully with any fruits, ranging from tart to sweet. When using fresh produce for a secondary ferment, it is necessary to swap it out every 24 hours. Follow the method to do this and it's a super simple procedure.

24 raspberries, divided
4 cups of finished plain water kefir, grains removed
1 lemon

1. In a clean 1-quart jar, combine 12 of the raspberries and the water kefir.

2. Cut the lemon in half, and squeeze all of its juice into the jar. Cover the jar with a lid, and leave the contents to ferment for 24 hours in a warm location.

3. The following day, prepare a new 1-quart jar. Pour the water kefir through a funnel topped with a wire mesh strainer and into the other jar. Add the remaining 12 raspberries. Cover and close the jar, leaving it to ferment for 24 hours in a warm location.

4. Prepare two 12-ounce swing-top bottles (or their equivalent) in which to bottle the water kefir. Using a strainer set atop a funnel, fill the bottles and then seal them. Leave the bottles in a warm location for 24 hours to build additional carbonation. Refrigerate until ready to serve.

TRY INSTEAD

Use some of your Blackberry Shrub (page 165) or any other shrub you make to flavor your water kefir for a sweet-and-sour tweak that will wake up your taste buds. When adding shrub syrup or fruit juices to water kefir for a secondary fermentation, use about ½ cup per quart of water kefir. Limit secondary fermentation to 2 to 3 days, especially when fermenting in a tightly closed vessel, such as a swing-top bottle.

BREWS

10

BEET KVASS

MAKES: 1 QUART **PREP TIME**: 5 MINUTES **FERMENTATION TIME**: 2 TO 7 DAYS

BEGINNER

This beverage has a long history in Eastern Europe. Not only can this nutritious living drink be consumed raw, but it can also be added to soups and vinaigrettes for a tasty, healthy boost. Beets, known for their liver-cleansing properties, are thought to have positive effects on certain long-term conditions, such as chronic fatigue, allergies, and many different types of digestive problems.

2 medium-size beets
2 tablespoons whey (page 23)
    or sauerkraut juice
1 tablespoon sea salt
Water

1. Wash the beets thoroughly. If they are organic, leave the skins on, but if they are not, peel the skins off. Dice them into chunks no larger than 1 inch across, and place them in a quart jar.

2. Add the whey or sauerkraut juice and salt to the container, and fill the jar with water.

3. Cover the jar with a clean kitchen towel secured with a rubber band. Leave the jar in a warm location for 2 to 7 days. Once bubbles begin rising rapidly, the kvass is ready for drinking.

4. Remove the kitchen towel, place a lid on the jar, and transfer it to the refrigerator.

A CLOSER LOOK

For a second batch of a slightly weaker kvass, save your beets and reuse them. Place the already-used beets in a clean jar, add about 1 cup of finished kvass as a starter, and add the same amount of salt and water as in the preceding recipe to create a lighter version of the drink. Once bubbles reappear in the kvass, it is ready to be consumed.

PEACH KVASS

MAKES: 1 QUART **PREP TIME:** 5 MINUTES **FERMENTATION TIME:** 2 DAYS

BEGINNER

Beets are not the only kvass out there! You can make a sweet, flavored kvass with just about any fruit you can think of and enjoy this slightly fermented concoction in place of sugary beverages. Simple to make, this traditional drink can be explored in your own kitchen. If your favorite fresh fruits are not in season, thaw some frozen produce and get to making this scrumptious treat!

2 medium-size peaches
1 tablespoon honey
1 thumb-size piece of ginger, sliced
Water

1. Wash the peaches thoroughly. Cut the peaches in half and remove the pits. Dice the pieces into chunks or cut into wedges, and place them in a 1-quart jar. Add the honey and ginger. Fill the jar with water, leaving at least an inch of headspace in the top of the jar.

2. Cover the jar with a lid, and leave it in a warm location for 2 days to ferment. Shake the jar once a day to redistribute the ingredients, and open it once daily to allow gas to escape.

3. After 2 days, place the lid tightly on the jar, and transfer it to the refrigerator, where it will keep for 1 week.

FERMENTED CARROT JUICE

MAKES: 1 QUART   **PREP TIME**: 10 MINUTES
FERMENTATION TIME: 3 DAYS, PLUS 1 WEEK COLD STORAGE

BEGINNER

Carrots are similar to beets in that they can stay in the ground in their own personal cold storage system until needed. Before the weather turns cold and the ground freezes, when you want to get your carrots out of the ground, you might find yourself with a crazy abundance. If so, here is another way to put the beta-carotene-rich carrots to use. This recipe requires a juicer, and with nothing more than salt and carrot juice you can create a succulent beverage that's great for everyday drinking or as a remedy when you're getting over a sickness.

1 quart carrot juice
2 teaspoons sea salt

Pour the juice into a jar and mix the salt in well. Cover with a lid and store at room temperature for 3 days before transferring to cold storage for at least 1 week or up to 4 weeks before serving.

TRY INSTEAD

This method can also be used with beet juice to create an alternative to beet kvass, a thicker fermentation. The catch is that this technique requires a juicer, making the traditional beet kvass a better option for people without one. But if you can find fresh-pressed vegetable juices near you, they can also be used for these recipes.

BREWS

10

BLACKBERRY SHRUB

MAKES: 1 QUART **PREP TIME**: 15 MINUTES **FERMENTATION TIME**: 8 DAYS

BEGINNER

A shrub is a simple syruplike ferment. For a family-friendly treat, mix a shrub with a little sparkling water or even water kefir to create a fruity, sodalike beverage. Shrubs make a great addition to a number of cocktails, adding both sweet and sour notes, which complement countless combinations of liquors, mixers, and other flavors. Start with blackberries, but feel free to go from there and use whatever else you have in your fruit supply. Because mashing is required to release some juices from the fruit, berries are always a great choice for making shrubs.

1 cup blackberries
1 cup apple cider vinegar
¾ cup sugar

1. Put the blackberries into a jar. Using a pestle or other kitchen tool, smash the berries lightly to release their juices and break them up.

2. Pour the vinegar into the jar and stir. Cover with a clean kitchen towel, and leave at room temperature overnight.

3. The following day, add the sugar to the jar and stir well until combined. Cap tightly with a lid, and refrigerate the shrub for 7 days before using. If desired, strain out the fruit bits before mixing with other drinks.

TRY INSTEAD

Shrubs are highly customizable and a great way to infuse some additional herbs and spices into your everyday diet. When using whole spices, such as fresh ginger, slice pieces and bruise them gently with a pestle to release juices. To add herbs, such as mint, rosemary, lemongrass, or lemon balm, tear or lightly bruise the leaves in the same way to release their oils for a stronger infusion.

HARD APPLE CIDER

MAKES: 1 GALLON **PREP TIME:** 5 MINUTES, 20 MINUTES FOR BOTTLING
FERMENTATION TIME: 12 TO 21 DAYS

BEGINNER

Hard apple cider is one of the easiest and oldest alcoholic fermented beverages around. You could actually just leave a jar of unpasteurized apple cider undisturbed, and it would naturally turn into alcohol. For a little more control and a tastier finished product, use commercial yeast to create this brew that will have you wishing apples were always in season. You will need a 1-gallon carboy, bung, and air lock for this recipe, as well as some bottles in which to store the finished cider. For easier transfer of the finished beverage, plastic tubing and an auto-siphon designed to move wine and beer are handy and inexpensive items to have on hand.

1 gallon fresh-pressed, unpasteurized apple cider
1 envelope cider or champagne yeast

1. Pour the cider into the carboy, leaving a few inches of headspace. Add the yeast, cap the carboy, and give it a gentle shake to disperse it throughout the liquid. Depending on the type of yeast, it may need hydration before being added to the cider; if necessary, follow package instructions before adding to the cider.

2. Fill the air lock to the indicated fill line with water and replace its cap. Affix the air lock to the bung and then to the carboy.

3. Place the mixture in a cool, dark location for 7 to 14 days. Taste the cider once or twice during this time to gauge its progress. It will gradually become less sweet, and you can use your own judgment on when it is complete to your liking. If you plan on keeping the cider in bottles, the drink should be very low in sugar. The cider will continue to ferment in bottles, and if it is too sweet, too much pressure can build, causing an explosion.

4. Transfer the cider to bottles using plastic tubing and an auto-siphon to prevent disturbing the bottom sediment. If you don't have tubing, carefully pour the cider into bottles using a funnel. If using this method, be sure to set up all the bottles before beginning, so that you do not have to keep setting the carboy down between each bottle, as this will cause the sediment to disperse and create a cloudy cider.

5. Affix tops to the bottles, and store them for 5 to 7 more days at room temperature to create carbonation, before refrigerating and serving cold.

MEAD

MAKES: 1 GALLON **PREP TIME**: 10 MINUTES **FERMENTATION TIME**: 2 WEEKS TO 1 MONTH

BEGINNER

Mead, or honey wine, is one of the most traditional fermented beverages. Although raw honey naturally inhibits microbial activity on its own, raw honey diluted with water will easily turn into a delightful, mildly sweet wine perfect for an after-dinner drink. You will need a 1-gallon carboy, an air lock and bung, and bottles for storage. Plastic tubing and an auto-siphon also make transferring the mead much easier.

9 cups water
4 cups honey
1 envelope champagne yeast

1. Bring the water to a boil and turn off the heat. Stir in the honey until dissolved. Let the mixture cool to at least 100°F before proceeding.

2. Pour the honey-water mixture into the 1-gallon carboy. Sprinkle the yeast onto the surface, affix the top, and gently shake the carboy to mix the yeast into the honey-water. Depending on the type of yeast you use, you may need to rehydrate it first. If this is necessary, follow package directions to do this before adding the yeast to the honey-water mixture.

3. Fill the air lock with water to the fill line and affix its top. Place the air lock in a bung and then the bung into the carboy to create a seal. Place the jug in a cool, dark location.

4. After about 2 weeks, test the mead to determine its doneness. If it is good, it is finished. If not, allow it to proceed until it reaches a nice balance of alcohol and sweetness. For a still mead, you will want to ferment it until no noticeable sugar is present. Once the mead is bottled, if sugar is still present, this will create carbonation in the finished product.

Continued

BREWS

10

5. Transfer the mead to prepared swing-top bottles using plastic tubing and an auto-siphon, being careful not to disturb the sediment. Without tubing, carefully pour the mead into prepared bottles slowly and evenly to prevent disturbing the sediment.

6. Cap the bottles and store them until ready for drinking.

A CLOSER LOOK

Although the sediment on the bottom of a brew may look scary, don't worry about this oozing mixture. Composed largely of dead yeast cells, this mixture is not harmful. For taste and quality reasons, you want to avoid it. But if you do happen to get some into a bottle, allow it to settle upright. When serving, pour the mead into another glass slowly, leaving the last bit of mead and sediment in the bottle.

BREWS

10

GINGER BEER

MAKES: 2 QUARTS **PREP TIME:** 10 MINUTES, 5 MINUTES DAILY FOR UP TO 7 DAYS
FERMENTATION TIME: 3 TO 7 DAYS FOR STARTER, 7 TO 11 DAYS FOR GINGER BEER

INTERMEDIATE

Ginger beer is a popular and refreshing beverage enjoyed throughout the world. Despite its name, ginger beer is not alcoholic. Instead, it is a highly effervescent beverage that is as much a tonic as it is a treat on a hot day. Known for its stomach-soothing abilities, it shines here in a slightly spicy and spectacularly fizzy ferment. To create ginger beer, you will first need to make a starter to get fermentation going strong.

FOR THE GINGER STARTER

1 cup water

1 teaspoon sugar, plus additional sugar for feeding starter

1 teaspoon grated ginger, plus additional ginger for feeding starter

FOR THE GINGER BEER

7 cups water

¾ cup sugar

3 tablespoons freshly squeezed lemon juice

3 tablespoons grated ginger

1. Create the ginger starter by adding 1 cup of water to a small jar. Add 1 teaspoon sugar and 1 teaspoon grated ginger, and stir until the sugar is dissolved. Cover the jar with a clean kitchen towel secured by a rubber band. Wrap the jar with another towel around the sides to help insulate it, and then place the starter in a warm location, about 75°F to 85°F.

2. After 24 hours, you will need to begin feeding the starter. Place an additional 1½ teaspoons of sugar and 1 teaspoon of grated ginger into the jar, and stir well with a clean utensil. Continue this process every day for the next 3 to 7 days, until it begins fizzing. When it is actively bubbling, stop feeding the starter and proceed.

3. To make the ginger beer, put the 7 cups of water into a half-gallon jar. Add the sugar and freshly squeezed lemon juice to the water, and stir well to dissolve the sugar. Add ½ cup of the ginger starter and the remaining grated ginger. Reserve the leftover ginger starter for possible later use. Stir well and cover the jar with a clean kitchen towel secured with a rubber band.

Continued

BREWS

10

4. Wrap the sides of the jar with a thick kitchen towel, and place it in a warm location, where it can maintain a temperature of 75°F to 85°F. Stir the mixture every 2 days, tasting it after day 4. By this time, there should be bubbles in the ferment. If not, add the reserved ginger starter.

5. Once bubbles are actively appearing, transfer the ginger beer to swing-top bottles to help build carbonation; pour the ginger beer into the bottles through a strainer set over a funnel. Cap the containers and leave them on the counter for 3 to 5 days. Refrigerate and serve when desired. Because the sugar in the ginger beer will continue to be consumed by bacteria and yeast, drinking it within the first 3 weeks of production allows you to enjoy the most sweetness and pronounced flavor in the finished beverage.

BREWS

10

FERMENTED ALMOND MILK

MAKES: 1 QUART **PREP TIME:** 20 MINUTES, OVERNIGHT SOAK **FERMENTATION TIME:** 2 DAYS

INTERMEDIATE

Store-bought almond milk contains many additives, which may concern you if you explore them a bit. When you make fermented almond milk yourself, you have the peace of mind that you are serving your family a clean product with nothing nasty. Use this tasty treat as a replacement for dairy milk, or simply drink a glass for filling nourishment.

1 cup almonds
Water
1 teaspoon sea salt
2 tablespoons freshly squeezed lemon juice
2 tablespoons honey
1 teaspoon almond extract

1. Bring a pot of water to a boil and add the almonds. Blanch for 1 minute and then remove them promptly with a strainer. Transfer the almonds to a colander, and rinse with cold water for about a minute until cool. Use your fingers to slip the almonds out of their skins, placing the nuts in a separate jar as you go.

2. Cover the almonds with water and add the salt, stirring to dissolve. Put a lid on the jar, and leave them to soak overnight.

3. Drain the nuts and transfer them into a food processor or blender. Process them until they are a smooth paste.

4. Transfer the paste into a 1-quart jar. Add the remaining ingredients and enough water to fill the jar. Stir well and cover the jar with a lid. Place in a warm location to ferment for 2 days. Transfer to the refrigerator to cool. If desired, strain before serving.

A CLOSER LOOK

Although almonds are a high-fat food, they can be a regular part of a healthy diet. Loaded with monounsaturated fat, these slightly sweet nuts have been linked to many health benefits, such as lowering both LDL cholesterol and the risk of heart disease. Packed with vitamin E, magnesium, and potassium, they can be a great replacement for dairy milk when prepared in this way.

BREWS

10

RED WINE

MAKES: 1 GALLON **PREP TIME:** 15 MINUTES
FERMENTATION TIME: 5 TO 7 WEEKS, UP TO 1 MORE MONTH TO CLEAR

ADVANCED

To get your "feet wet" in wine making, start by making wine from a bottled grape juice or grape juice concentrate found at your local grocery store. This simple method skips over the time-consuming crushing and pressing of fresh grapes and allows you to try your hand at making a one-gallon batch without fancy equipment. Be sure to check the label and use a grape juice that has no added preservatives, such as sodium benzoate or potassium sorbate, which would interfere with fermentation. You will need two 1-gallon jugs, a bung and air lock, a food-grade plastic bucket that is 1½ gallons or larger, an auto-siphon, and plastic tubing for this recipe. Find all the ingredients other than the juice at a local home brew shop or check out our Resources section (page 193) for online sources.

2 (64-ounce) jugs of dark grape juice
½ pound cane sugar
1 teaspoon yeast nutrient
¾ teaspoon acid blend
⅛ teaspoon tannin
2 Campden tablets, divided
1 package red wine yeast

1. Clean and sanitize the food-grade bucket. Pour the juice, sugar, yeast nutrient, acid blend, and tannin into the juice, and stir with a clean plastic spoon until the sugar is dissolved. Crush the first Campden tablet, add it to the juice, and stir. Cover the bucket with a clean kitchen towel or clean pillowcase, and let it sit undisturbed for 24 hours in a warm location with a temperature between 70°F and 75°F.

2. Sprinkle the wine yeast over the surface of the juice. Cover the bucket again and leave it to ferment for 5 days.

3. Using the tubing and auto-siphon, siphon the juice into a cleaned and sanitized 1-gallon jug. There will be a good deal of sediment in the bottom of the container, and you want to get some into the new jug.

4. Fill an air lock to the line with water, affix its top, and insert it into the bung. Press the bung into the opening of the jug. Leave it undisturbed for 4 to 6 weeks.

5. At this time, test the wine using a hydrometer to verify the sugar content. When the wine is complete, it will have a specific gravity between 0.990 and 0.998, and at that point, the wine is done fermenting. Add the remaining crushed Campden tablet.

6. Siphon the wine again into the other cleaned and sanitized 1-gallon jug using the plastic tubing and auto-siphon. Leave behind all sediment. The wine should be fairly clear at this point. If it is not, leave it to sit undisturbed for 3 to 4 more weeks and re-rack it back into the other 1-gallon jug before drinking.

USING A HYDROMETER

A hydrometer is a simple tool and can accurately measure how much sugar is in a liquid. To use it, always begin by cleaning and sanitizing it and the testing jar. Once complete, fill the testing jar with a liquid. Carefully lower the hydrometer into the jar with your thumb and index finger. Before you release it into the liquid, give it a spin with your fingers so that it floats evenly in the liquid and does not rest against the wall of the testing jar. You can take a reading by looking at where the liquid falls on the scale at its center point.

For wine and beer making, you will use two scales on the hydrometer—the potential alcohol scale (or Brix scale) and the specific gravity scale. The Brix scale can be used at the beginning of fermentation to quickly assess how much alcohol your brew will have in it if it is fermented to dryness, meaning there is no sugar left in the beverage.

The specific gravity scale can be used to determine how much sugar remains in a ferment. Typically wines are transferred to a secondary fermenter, where oxygen is not present, when the wine reaches below .998 on the specific gravity scale.

11

COOKING WITH FERMENTED FOODS

D on't let all your carefully fermented foods just sit there—use them! Get to know all the new textures and flavors of these products, and incorporate them into your everyday cooking to infuse some serious creativity into your meal preparation. Fresh is always best when you are mainly interested in the probiotic benefits, as cooking kills beneficial bacteria. But cooking with fermented foods can add exciting variety to your meals.

FERMENTED BERRY AND CREAM SMOOTHIE

MAKES: 1 SMOOTHIE **PREP TIME:** 5 MINUTES

BEGINNER

Nothing makes an early rise easier than an energizing smoothie. Chock-full of nutrients that will saturate your body with vitamins and minerals, this smoothie is the perfect way to start your day the probiotic way. Skip your morning coffee and fill up with this coconut and berry smoothie to keep you powered up all morning long.

1 cup water
1 cup dried, shredded, unsweetened coconut
1 cup Lacto-Fermented Berries (page 70)
1 apple, chopped
1 cup tightly packed spinach

Add the water, coconut, berries, apple, and spinach to a blender. Process until smooth, about 30 to 60 seconds. Serve immediately.

KIMCHI OMELET

MAKES: 1 OMELET **PREP TIME:** 10 MINUTES **COOK TIME:** 5 MINUTES

BEGINNER

If you have never had a kimchi omelet, you must try this recipe. Salty and spicy, kimchi pairs well with eggs to create this quick, dairy-free meal that comes together in minutes. With just a few ingredients and minimal prep time, you can make use of some of that extra kimchi you have lying around (if there still is any). If not, get a batch started, and begin serving this at breakfast to get a jump-start on a probiotic-filled day.

2 large eggs

Salt

Pepper

½ teaspoon mirin (rice wine)

1 teaspoon vegetable oil

1 scallion, cut into rounds

3 tablespoons chopped Kimchi (page 39)

2 or 3 mushrooms, sliced (optional)

¼ cup peas (optional)

1. Crack the eggs into a bowl, and season lightly with salt and pepper. Add the mirin and mix well.

2. Heat the oil in a skillet over medium-high heat, and sauté the scallion, kimchi, and any other vegetables (if using) for 2 minutes.

3. Pour the eggs into the skillet and cover. Cook for an additional 2 to 3 minutes, until the egg is set.

4. Open the lid and, using a spatula, fold the omelet in half and serve. Top with additional kimchi or Asian-style hot sauce if desired.

TRY INSTEAD

Kimchi is the main flavoring in this omelet, but that doesn't mean it can't include your favorite vegetables, too. Add sliced zucchini, tomatoes, summer squash, or greens such as spinach, Swiss chard, or kale to increase the nutritional value of this meal.

COOKING WITH FERMENTED FOODS

11

KEFIR BISCUITS

MAKES: 10 BISCUITS **PREP TIME:** 15 MINUTES **COOK TIME:** 12 TO 14 MINUTES

BEGINNER

If you are making kefir regularly, you can sometimes get behind in drinking it, and it begins to pile up in your refrigerator. These biscuits are a great way to make use of extra kefir; using a mix of whole wheat and white flour, the biscuits are healthier than store-bought and leave out additional preservatives. Serve these with fermented jam and eggs prepared in your favorite style for a breakfast done right.

1 cup whole wheat flour
1 cup unbleached all-purpose flour
2 teaspoons baking powder
½ teaspoon baking soda
1 teaspoon sugar
½ teaspoon salt
8 tablespoons cold butter
¾ cup Kefir (page 79)

1. Preheat your oven to 450°F.

2. Mix the flours, baking powder, baking soda, sugar, and salt in a large bowl.

3. Cut the butter into small squares, and cut into the flour using a pastry blender or two forks until the butter is all in small pieces and the mixture resembles wet sand.

4. Add the kefir and stir the mixture with a spoon until it comes together. Use your hands to finish mixing it, integrating all the little pieces and giving it several turns with your hands to create a firm, slightly sticky dough. If it is overly sticky, add a little more flour.

5. Divide the dough into small balls a little larger than a golf ball, shaping them with your hands. Press each ball lightly onto a rimmed baking sheet to slightly flatten it.

6. Bake the biscuits for 12 to 14 minutes until well browned. Serve promptly while still warm.

TRY INSTEAD

Kefir gives these biscuits a distinctive taste, but you can easily substitute yogurt or cultured buttermilk here. Use the same amount of either when substituting to create equally delicious biscuits.

OATMEAL PANCAKES

MAKES: 8 TO 10 PANCAKES **PREP TIME:** 10 MINUTES

BEGINNER

When you make Soaked Oatmeal (page 95), save your leftovers and try these simple pancakes the next morning. By preparing large batches of fermented oats, you can quickly whip up a batch of these pancakes on a busy morning.

2 cups leftover Soaked Oatmeal

1 cup milk

2 eggs

¾ cup all-purpose flour

2 teaspoons baking powder

3 to 4 tablespoons butter, divided

Maple syrup, for serving

1. Mix the leftover oatmeal with the milk, eggs, flour, and baking powder to create a batter.

2. Heat the butter in a large skillet. Use half to grease the skillet, and stir the other half into the pancake batter. Drop the pancake batter onto the skillet in large spoonfuls to create several pancakes at a time. Cook until bubbles begin to form on the surface, and flip; 3 to 4 minutes per side will get them nice and golden brown. Serve warm with maple syrup.

HOMEMADE GRANOLA WITH BERRIES AND YOGURT

MAKES: 1 QUART **PREP TIME:** 15 MINUTES

BEGINNER

Making granola is one thing that doesn't have to be a chore. With this stream-lined overnight granola recipe, you can mix the ingredients, cook them, and turn off the oven to let it do its work. By morning, your crunchy, delicious granola awaits you, ready to be smothered in lacto-fermented berries and yogurt. Add a spoonful of honey to sweeten things up a bit and enjoy this quick breakfast on a busy morning.

7 cups old-fashioned oats

2 teaspoons ground cinnamon

¼ teaspoon salt

½ cup applesauce

½ cup honey

¼ cup canola oil

2 teaspoons vanilla extract

Yogurt, for serving (page 87)

Lacto-Fermented Berries, for serving (page 70)

1. Preheat the oven to 375°F. Measure the oats into a large bowl, and toss with the cinnamon and salt until well mixed.

2. Combine the applesauce, honey, canola oil, and vanilla extract in another bowl and mix well. Pour the wet mixture into the oats and stir well. Spread the mixture on a rimmed baking sheet, and place in the oven.

3. Bake the granola for 10 minutes. Turn off the oven, leaving the pan in it overnight.

4. In the morning, break up the granola into small pieces and store in an airtight container.

5. Serve topped with a generous scoop of home-made yogurt and berries.

THE ULTIMATE SALAD

MAKES: 2 LARGE DINNER SALADS OR 4 SIDE SALADS **PREP TIME**: 15 MINUTES

BEGINNER

When you make fermented foods regularly, you begin to see how they can be added to just about everything you cook to boost probiotic value and flavor. This salad is simple to throw together, and when topped with a piece of salmon or chicken, it can be a meal on its own. When fermented, garlic mellows substantially, allowing you to add more to your meals without a strong residual odor. For added zing, slice some pieces of Salmon (page 131) to top the salad and call it lunch.

6 to 8 cups torn salad greens (a mixture of romaine, arugula, spinach, butter lettuce, and red leaf lettuces works well)

2 tablespoons olive oil

3 to 5 Fermented Garlic cloves (page 150)

½ teaspoon salt

¼ teaspoon freshly ground black pepper

1 lemon

1. Wash the salad greens well, and remove any pieces that are wilted or have brown edges. Use a salad spinner to remove excess water, or place the leaves in a colander lined with plenty of paper towels and let dry. To remove more liquid, shake the salad greens around several times as they sit.

2. Pour the olive oil into a large bowl. Using a large knife, crush the garlic by placing the knife on the bowl, holding it in place with one hand, and hitting the side of the blade with your opposite palm. Lift the knife and chop the garlic into small pieces. Add this to the olive oil.

3. Add the greens to the bowl, and stir together using a large spoon to coat them evenly. Sprinkle the salt and pepper over the greens and mix again.

4. Cut the lemon in half, and using a small strainer to catch any seeds, squeeze all the juice from the lemon into the salad. Mix well, add salt and pepper, and serve.

TRY INSTEAD

For a different flavor, omit the lemon juice and instead add 1 to 2 tablespoons of homemade Red Wine Vinegar (page 143), Apple Cider Vinegar (page 141), or Fruit Vinegar (page 144). Include any desired vegetables or fruits, such as cucumbers, red or green peppers, banana peppers, shredded carrots, or berries. For a little more zing, add a couple of tablespoons of shredded Lacto-Fermented Carrot Spears (page 47) to the salad.

COOKING WITH FERMENTED FOODS

11

SOURED LENTIL SOUP

MAKES: 8 CUPS **PREP TIME:** 10 MINUTES **COOK TIME:** 30 MINUTES

BEGINNER

A perfect meal on cool days, lentil soup is a trifecta of goodness—filling, nutritious, and warming all at once. Pancetta adds a deep, meaty flavor to the soup. And fermented lentils give the finished soup a characteristically fermented feel, while the vegetables enhance its vitamin content. Serve with a nice salad or warm bread.

4 slices of Pancetta (page 136)

1 large onion, chopped

2 cups lacinato kale, steams and center rims discarded and leaves chopped

2 cups cabbage, chopped

16 oz soy beans

2 cups Soured Lentils (page 111)

6 cups chicken stock

½ teaspoon salt

½ teaspoon freshly ground black pepper

2 teaspoons ground cumin

1. Chop the pancetta into small pieces, and place in a large pot over medium-high heat. Cook until crispy. Remove using a slotted spoon and set aside. Pour off all but 2 tablespoons of the rendered fat in the pot.

2. Sauté the onions in the fat until tender and the onion becomes translucent.

3. Add the lentils, soy beans, chicken stock, salt, pepper, cumin, and reserved pancetta to the pan. Bring to a boil and simmer for 10 minutes, stirring occasionally. Add the kale and cabbage and continue to simmer for 10 more minutes.

4. Add more water if the soup becomes too thick to create your desired consistency. Adjust seasonings with additional salt and pepper, as needed.

CREAMY VEGETABLE SOUP

MAKES: 3 QUARTS **PREP TIME:** 10 MINUTES **COOK TIME:** 30 MINUTES

BEGINNER

Creating a great bowl of soup is an important culinary craft. Top this bowl of liquid goodness with kefir cheese, and you have a savory, satiating masterpiece.

4 tablespoons canola oil

2 onions, chopped

2 carrots, chopped

6 red or gold potatoes, diced

8 cups chicken stock or vegetable stock

4 sprigs thyme

4 sprigs flat-leaf parsley

½ teaspoon peppercorns

4 zucchini, sliced

Sea salt

Pepper

Kefir Cheese, for serving (page 86)

1. Heat the oil in a large pot, and add the onions and carrots to the pot. Sauté until the onions become translucent.

2. Add the potatoes to the pot and stir a few times. Pour in the stock and bring it to a boil. Reduce the heat to simmer. Tie the thyme and parsley together using kitchen twine and add to the pot, along with the peppercorns. Simmer for about 15 minutes, or until the potatoes are tender.

3. Add the zucchini slices and simmer for 5 more minutes. Remove the herbs from the pot. Use an immersion blender to purée the soup, or transfer it to a blender to process until smooth.

4. Season with salt and pepper.

5. Top with kefir cheese crumbles and serve hot.

SAUERKRAUT SLOW COOKER DIP

MAKES: 1 QUART **PREP TIME:** 15 MINUTES **COOK TIME:** 3 TO 5 HOURS

BEGINNER

Forget about traditional nachos—open up a jar of sauerkraut next time you want to make a great tortilla chip topper for the big game. This super easy, set-it-and-forget-it slow cooker recipe will have even those who don't like sauerkraut dipping their chips in it. Using simple, readily available ingredients, prepare this creamy, filling dip in a matter of minutes, and have it ready to go for game time.

1 pound ground beef or turkey

4 tomatoes, chopped

3 green peppers, chopped

4 cups Sauerkraut (page 34), drained

1 ½ cups sour cream

1. Brown the ground meat in a skillet and drain away the fat.

2. Add all the ingredients to a slow cooker, and cook on low for 3 to 5 hours. Stir and serve with tortilla chips.

LAMB DOLMAS

MAKES: 30 DOLMAS **PREP TIME:** 45 MINUTES **COOK TIME:** 30 MINUTES

INTERMEDIATE

Preparing dolmas can be a time-consuming task, but if you set up your workstation right, you can make quick work out of it. Mix the filling first and then lay out as many grape leaves on your counter as will fit. Stuff each with a bit of the mixed filling and roll them up. Repeat this bulk stuffing process a couple of times, and you'll be done before you know it. Make dolmas ahead of time, as they keep well refrigerated for two days. To serve, warm them up in a pan with a little water or serve them at room temperature.

½ cup basmati or another long-grained rice
2 tablespoons butter
1 onion, chopped
2 garlic cloves, minced
½ teaspoon ground allspice
½ teaspoon ground cinnamon
½ teaspoon freshly ground black pepper
½ pound ground lamb
¼ cup pine nuts
¼ cup dried cranberries
½ tablespoon salt
30 Pickled Grape Leaves (page 50)
¾ cup olive oil
Juice of 2 lemons
Yogurt, for serving (page 87)

1. Pour the rice into a bowl and cover with water. Soak for 30 minutes and drain.

2. While the rice is soaking, melt the butter in a skillet. Add the onions and cook until tender and translucent. Add the garlic and spices, and cook for 2 to 4 minutes more. Cool the mixture for a few minutes.

3. In a bowl, combine the onion mixture, ground lamb, pine nuts, cranberries, and salt. When ready, mix in the drained rice.

Continued

COOKING WITH FERMENTED FOODS

11

4. Pull the grape leaves out of the jar carefully so that they are not ripped. Unwrap the leaves and snip off any protruding stems. Rinse them with cool water, and pat them dry with a clean kitchen towel. Lay several grape leaves, smooth side down, on a clean counter.

5. With clean hands, take a tablespoon-size piece of the mixture, shape it into a cylindrical shape, and place it near the stem of a leaf. Repeat this step until all the leaves are topped. Turn both sides of a leaf inward, and starting at the bottom, roll the grape leaf up and away from you into a cylinder. During cooking the rice expands, so take care not to roll them too tight.

6. Arrange the dolmas in a large pot so that they fit snugly together with their seam sides down, in a single layer—if they don't fit in one pot, split them into two groups. Pour the olive and lemon juice over the dolmas. Use a plate with an additional weight placed on top of it to hold the dolmas in place and prevent them from unrolling while cooking.

7. Add just enough hot water to the pot to cover the dolmas. Heat the water-oil mixture to boiling, cover the pot, and reduce the heat. Simmer the dolmas for 30 minutes. Uncover the pot and remove the plate. When cool enough to handle, use a spatula to remove them and arrange on a plate for serving. Serve with fresh yogurt for dipping.

UDON NOODLE SOUP

MAKES: 2 SERVINGS **PREP TIME:** 10 MINUTES **COOK TIME:** 15 MINUTES

INTERMEDIATE

A perfect dish for a cold winter night, this udon noodle soup is soothing and warming. This is a relatively quick meal to throw together on a busy night or weekday. This soup is meant to be served piping hot. If desired, add more vegetables to customize this flavorful dish.

½ pound dried udon noodles

4 green onions

4 dried mushrooms

4 cups chicken stock or broth

⅓ cup Soy Sauce (page 124)

⅓ cup mirin (rice wine)

1 teaspoon salt

2 teaspoons sugar

2 eggs

1 cup cooked chicken breast, shredded

1. Boil the noodles in water until soft. Drain and run under cool water to chill. Divide the noodles into two bowls.

2. Cut the green onions into 2-inch-long batons. Soak the mushrooms in hot water in a small bowl. When reconstituted, cut each into several slices.

3. Make the broth by adding the chicken stock, soy sauce, mirin, salt, and sugar to the pot and bringing it to a simmer. Turn off the heat. Carefully crack each egg into the broth so that they remain intact. Do not stir. Cover the pot and let sit until the whites of the eggs are set, or about 6 minutes.

4. Using a ladle, remove each egg from the broth, and place one in each bowl on the bed of noodles. Pour the broth over the noodles. Split the green onions, chicken, and mushrooms between the two bowls, arrange them atop the noodles, and serve hot.

TRY INSTEAD

This recipe can also be made with Miso (page 118) for a different flavor. Add ¼ cup miso and cut the soy sauce to just 2 tablespoons to create a soup with a slightly nuttier taste. When cooking with miso, be sure not to bring the stock to a boil, to preserve the probiotic qualities of the ferment.

COOKING WITH FERMENTED FOODS

11

KOMBUCHA-BATTERED FRIED FISH
WITH HERBED YOGURT DIPPING SAUCE

MAKES: 4 SERVINGS **PREP TIME:** 15 MINUTES **COOK TIME:** 30 MINUTES

INTERMEDIATE

Kombucha-battered fish is a fun spin on the beer-battered pub favorite that creates a light, airy, and crisp batter with a whole lot of character. Use cod or another firm white fish for best results. Adventurous eaters can try frying all sorts of vegetables in this batter, too, such as fresh or fermented green beans, zucchini slices, cauliflower, and even pickles for a tasty meal accompaniment.

8 cups canola oil
1½ pounds cod (or another firm white fish)
1 cup all-purpose flour
1½ teaspoons coarse kosher or sea salt
½ teaspoon baking powder
1 cup plain kombucha
½ cup Yogurt (page 87)
2 tablespoons chopped parsley
2 teaspoons Dijon mustard
1 tablespoon freshly squeezed lemon juice
½ teaspoon horseradish sauce

1. Pour the oil into a deep pot or fryer, and set over a burner on medium-high. Place a frying thermometer in the oil and heat the oil to 350°F.

2. Prepare the fish by cutting it into 1-inch-by-3-inch pieces. Mix the flour, salt, and baking powder together in a bowl. Pour in the kombucha and mix until the flour is incorporated and the batter is smooth.

3. Line a large plate or sheet pan with paper towels and set aside. Pat the fish dry and lightly salt it before dipping each piece in the batter. Shake off excess batter and immediately place the fish in the hot oil. Deep-fry the fish, flipping it once, until it is crisp and browned (about 7 minutes per side). Adjust the heat as necessary to keep it at 350°F.

4. Using a mesh strainer, transfer the fish to the prepared paper towel–lined sheet to drain. Continue battering and frying the fish until it is all cooked.

5. Mix the yogurt, parsley, Dijon mustard, lemon juice, and horseradish sauce in a small bowl. Serve with the hot fried fish.

A CLOSER LOOK

If you do not have a deep-fry thermometer, test the oil by dripping a touch of the batter in it. If it immediately crisps and cooks, the oil is ready.

11

MASALA DOSA WITH COCONUT CHUTNEY

MAKES: 4 MASALA DOSAS **PREP TIME:** 10 MINUTES **COOK TIME:** 15 MINUTES

ADVANCED

Masala dosa is a South Indian specialty that can be served all day long. This simple meal, made of a pea-and-potato curry stuffed inside a dosa, is filling, savory comfort food at its best. When served with Coconut Chutney, the flavors combine to create a salty, sweet, spicy, and slightly funky masterpiece. It may take a while to master the art of dosa making, and your first batch may not turn out quite like the version at your favorite restaurant. But don't be discouraged—it will taste heavenly, no matter how it looks.

6 small potatoes

2 tablespoons canola oil

1 teaspoon mustard seeds

1 pinch asafetida

1 cup sliced onions

2 green chiles

1 thumb-size piece of ginger, peeled and minced

¼ teaspoon turmeric

½ teaspoon salt

4 prepared Dosas (page 116)

1 cup Coconut Chutney (page 149)

1. Cut the potatoes in quarters, and boil in a small pan filled with water until just tender. Drain the water. Once cool, slip the skins off and lightly mash so that large chunks are still present.

2. In a skillet, heat the oil until shimmering and add the mustard seeds. When they begin to sputter, add the asafetida and stir again. Quickly add the sliced onions, chiles, and ginger. Stir continuously until the onions become tender but don't brown.

3. Add the turmeric powder and salt. Stir in ½ cup of water and bring to a boil. Add the mashed potatoes and cook for 5 to 6 more minutes until well blended and the water is absorbed. Turn off the heat.

4. Prepare the Dosas, and fill each with a large scoop of the potato mixture. Serve warm with Coconut Chutney for dipping.

THE DIRTY DOZEN & THE CLEAN FIFTEEN

A nonprofit and environmental watchdog organization called Environmental Working Group (EWG) looks at data supplied by the US Department of Agriculture (USDA) and the Food and Drug Administration (FDA) about pesticide residues and compiles a list each year of the best and worst pesticide loads found in commercial crops. You can use these lists to decide which fruits and vegetables to buy organic to minimize your exposure to pesticides and which produce is considered safe enough to skip the organics. This does not mean they are pesticide-free, though, so wash these fruits and vegetables thoroughly.

These lists change every year, so make sure you look up the most recent before you fill your shopping cart. You'll find the most recent lists as well as a guide to pesticides in produce at EWG.org/FoodNews.

2015 DIRTY DOZEN

Apples	Peaches
Celery	Potatoes
Cherry tomatoes	Snap peas
Cucumbers	Spinach
Grapes	Strawberries
Nectarines	Sweet bell peppers

In addition to the Dirty Dozen, the EWG added other foods contaminated with highly toxic organo-phosphate insecticides:

Hot peppers	Kale/Collard Greens

2015 CLEAN FIFTEEN

Asparagus	Mangoes
Avocados	Onions
Cabbage	Papayas
Cantaloupe	Pineapples
Cauliflower	Sweet corn
Eggplant	Sweet peas (frozen)
Grapefruit	Sweet potatoes
Kiwis	

MEASUREMENT CONVERSIONS

VOLUME EQUIVALENTS (LIQUID)

US STANDARD	US STANDARD (OUNCES)	METRIC (APPROXIMATE)
2 tablespoons	1 fl. oz.	30 mL
¼ cup	2 fl. oz.	60 mL
½ cup	4 fl. oz.	120 mL
1 cup	8 fl. oz.	240 mL
1½ cups	12 fl. oz.	355 mL
2 cups or 1 pint	16 fl. oz.	475 mL
4 cups or 1 quart	32 fl. oz.	1 L
1 gallon	128 fl. oz.	4 L

OVEN TEMPERATURES

FAHRENHEIT (F)	CELSIUS (C) (APPROXIMATE)
250°	120°
300°	150°
325°	165°
350°	180°
375°	190°
400°	200°
425°	220°
450°	230°

VOLUME EQUIVALENTS (DRY)

US STANDARD	METRIC (APPROXIMATE)
⅛ teaspoon	0.5 mL
¼ teaspoon	1 mL
½ teaspoon	2 mL
¾ teaspoon	4 mL
1 teaspoon	5 mL
1 tablespoon	15 mL
¼ cup	59 mL
⅓ cup	79 mL
½ cup	118 mL
⅔ cup	156 mL
¾ cup	177 mL
1 cup	235 mL
2 cups or 1 pint	475 mL
3 cups	700 mL
4 cups or 1 quart	1 L

WEIGHT EQUIVALENTS

US STANDARD	METRIC (APPROXIMATE)
½ ounce	15 g
1 ounce	30 g
2 ounces	60 g
4 ounces	115 g
8 ounces	225 g
12 ounces	340 g
16 ounces or 1 pound	455 g

RESOURCES

BREWING SUPPLIES

Northern Brewer
www.northernbrewer.com.

F.H. Steinbart
www.fhsteinbart.com.

CULTURES

Cultures for Health
www.culturesforhealth.com
/natural-fermentation.html.

FERMENTING SUPPLIES

Cultures for Health
www.culturesforhealth.com
/natural-fermentation.html.

Mountain Feed and Farm Supply
www.mountainfeed.com/collections.

SPECIALTY GROCERS

Patel Brothers
www.patelbrothers.com

REFERENCES

Fuhrman, Joel, MD. "Beans: The Ideal Carbohydrate." Accessed December 11, 2014. www.drfuhrman.com/library/beans_the_ideal_carbohydrate.aspx.

The Harvard Medical School Family Health Guide. "The Health Benefits of Taking Probiotics." Accessed November 20, 2014. www.health.harvard.edu/fhg/updates/update0905c.shtml.

Parvez, S., K. A. Malik, S. Ah Kang, and H.-Y. Kim. "Probiotics and Their Fermented Food Products Are Beneficial for Health." *Journal of Applied Microbiology* 100: 1171–85. doi:10.1111/j.1365-2672.2006.02963.x.

Tufts University Gerald J. and Dorothy R. Friedman School of Nutrition Science and Policy. "Discover the Digestive Benefits of Fermented Foods." Accessed November 19, 2014. www.nutritionletter.tufts.edu/issues/10_2/current-articles/Discover-the-Digestive -Benefits-of-Fermented-Foods_1383-1.html.

RECIPE INDEX

INDEX

ABOUT THE AUTHOR

Katherine Green is a writer and food educator in Portland, OR. She is a fermentation geek, trained winemaker, and the former owner of Mama Green's Jam. She lives with her husband, two sons, and a flock of chickens.

ALSO IN THE DIY SERIES

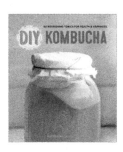

Steep-by-steep (and step-by-step) recipes to create your own fresh, fragrant, and fizzy kombucha.

AVAILABLE APRIL 2015
$12.99 paperback
$6.99 ebook

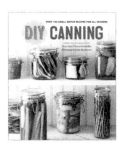

Preserve nature's bounty and enjoy seasonal ingredients throughout the year.

AVAILABLE APRIL 2015
$12.99 paperback
$6.99 ebook

CPSIA information can be obtained at www.ICGtesting.com
Printed in the USA
LVOW05s2230050815

448962LV00040B/180/P